A NEW OWNER'S
GUIDE TO
SCOTTISH TERRIERS

JG-137

Overleaf: A Scottish Terrier adult and puppy.

Opposite page: Ch. Charthill Oak Forest, owned by Charla Hill.

The publisher wishes to acknowledge the following owners of the dogs in this book: Joe Barnett, Dawn and Joel Bates, Lois Bolding, Jackie and Marvin Burton, Mary Dyer, Ron and Helen Girling, Robert Harley, Charla Hill, J. H. Ludlow, Dr. Barbara Anderson Lounsbury, John G. McPherson, Josephine Musson, Miriam Stamm, Robin Starr, Linda Terry, and Donna Winslow.

Photographers: A. Baker, Dawn and Joel Bates, Lois Bolding, CALLEA, Isabelle Francais, Robert Harley, Charla Hill, Dr. Barbara Anderson Lounsbury, Josephine Musson, S. Nute, Peggy O'Neil, Pets by Paulette, Shutter Pup, Miriam Stamm, Robin Starr, Donna Wislow, and Jill Andra Young.

The author acknowledges the contribution of Judy Iby for the following chapters in this book: Sport of Purebred Dogs, Health Care, Identification and Finding the Lost Dog, Traveling with Your Dog, and Behavior and Canine Communication.

The portrayal of canine pet products in this book is for general instructive value only; the appearance of such products does not necessarily constitute an endorsement by the authors, the publisher, or the owners of the dogs portrayed in this book.

Dedication

To everyone throughout the world whose lives have been enriched by Scotland's rugged individualist.

Distributed in the UNITED STATES to the Pet Trade by T.F.H. Publications, Inc., One T.F.H. Plaza, Neptune City, NJ 07753; on the Internet at www.tfh.com; in CANADA Rolf C. Hagen Inc., 3225 Sartelon St. Laurent-Montreal Quebec H4R 1E8; Pet Trade by H & L Pet Supplies Inc., 27 Kingston Crescent, Kitchener, Ontario N2B 2T6; in ENGLAND by T.F.H. Publications, PO Box 15, Waterlooville PO7 6BQ; in AUSTRALIA AND THE SOUTH PACIFIC by T.F.H. (Australia), Pty. Ltd., Box 149, Brookvale 2100 N.S.W., Australia; in NEW ZEALAND by Brooklands Aquarium Ltd. 5 McGiven Drive, New Plymouth, RD1 New Zealand; in SOUTH AFRICA, Rolf C. Hagen S.A. (PTY.) LTD. P.O. Box 201199, Durban North 4016, South Africa; in Japan by T.F.H. Publications, Japan—Jiro Tsuda, 10-12-3 Ohjidai, Sakura, Chiba 285, Japan. Published by T.F.H. Publications, Inc.

MANUFACTURED IN THE
UNITED STATES OF AMERICA
BY T.F.H. PUBLICATIONS, INC.

A New Owner's Guide to
Scottish Terriers

Richard G. Beauchamp

AND

Miriam "Buffy" Stamm

Contents

1998

The Scottish Terrier's loving and happy disposition makes him the ideal family pet.

The Scottish Terrier has a regal and majestic bearing.

This lovely duo pose for a basket of holiday cheer.

The well-socialized Scottish Terrier gets along famously with other animals.

Choose a puppy that is alert and active, with bright eyes and a shining coat.

FOREWORD

We lived in an apartment during the war years. World War II had called my father overseas and my mother was employed by the Red Cross. Apartment living accommodated our family's erratic schedule during those hectic days, but it denied me the opportunity of having the dog I so desperately wanted.

My best friend at that time lived only a block away and he not only was able to have a dog, he had two! They were Scottish Terriers and their names were Bonnie and Clyde. (I didn't quite get the pun then, but I'm sure it was fully intended!)

Scottish Terriers are inquisitive and active companions.

My friend's father was also away in the service. His mother was employed on a full-time basis as well, so the two of us boys had to fill many lonely hours. We occupied our time by hiking and exploring every nook and cranny of the area in which we lived. Bonnie and Clyde accompanied us everywhere and helped us in and out of the many

wonderful adventures that can only be fully appreciated by two curious young boys and their dogs.

One day Bonnie gave birth to a litter of five puppies—all coal-black like their parents. I was determined I would have one of the puppies for my own, but no amount of persuading could convince my mother to intercede with the apartment manager. I remained "dogless." "Scottieless" would actually be more appropriate in that I was fully convinced there was no breed that could ever match the devotion and companionship

Two Scotties are twice as much fun as just one. Ch. Charthill South Pacific and Ch. Charthill Tiger Rose make a handsome pair.

that my friend's dogs gave us. I decided that some day I, too, would own and breed Scotties.

Somehow this never came to pass. But my appreciation for the breed never diminished and every time I have been called upon to judge the breed through the years I could not help but recall those happy days with Bonnie, Clyde, and my friend.

Maintaining my interest in the Scottish Terrier through the years permitted me to appreciate the great contributions Miriam "Buffy" Stamm had made to the progress of the breed through her Anstamm Scotties over the past four decades. Therefore, I was particularly pleased to be able to collaborate with her in preparing this book.

Buffy Stamm's involvement with the Scottish Terrier breed is as much a part of the breed's contemporary history as Scotland is with the breed's origins. In 1952 she purchased her first well-bred Scottie, Anstamm Cimarron, from Anthony "Tony" Stamm. Buffy and Tony began attending shows together and when "Cimmie" whelped her first litter, Tony helped the rapidly learning novice to pick the best puppy from the litter. That puppy was Buffy's first champion.

Tony taught the budding enthusiast the ropes of showing dogs, but Buffy successfully taught herself all of the breed's intricate grooming techniques. Her second champion was another Cimmie offspring, Heigh-Ho Great Gusto. In retrospect, Buffy appreciates what an exceptional little dog he was, probably ranking with some of her best.

Tony and Buffy were married in 1954 and in the following year she joined the Scottish Terrier Club of America. At that time the STCA was in the hands of just a few eastern breeders and handlers. The two national specialties were held in New York in February and Philadelphia in the fall. None of this gave the Scottie the national representation it deserved, nor did it give the STCA the valuable input of the breed's experienced and successful fanciers throughout the country.

Buffy Stamm worked tirelessly and successfully to expand the interests of the STCA so that it would truly represent the breed's national strength and character. During her years as a member of the Board of Directors of the STCA, Buffy served as vice president and Show Chairman, editor of the yearbook and editor of the American Kennel Club *Gazette* Scottie column.

For a short time after the death of her husband in 1974, Buffy carried on the Anstamm breeding program alone but eventually added two partners, Cindy Cooke and Linda Nolan,

who now share the Anstamm name and contribute heavily to its success.

While it is only in more recent years that Mrs. Stamm began to keep accurate records of how many Anstamm Scotties became

The Scottish Terrier is a wonderful dog that inspires lifelong devotion in those who own them.

The lovely wheaten Ch. Sandgreg's Sweet Luv makes a striking picture against the night skyline. She is one of the breed's top producing females.

champions, it is certain there are more than 208 title holders bearing the Anstamm prefix, including countless Specialty Show, Terrier Group, and all-breed Best in Show winners.

The top producing sire in the breed was Ch. Anstamm Happy Venture, who alone produced 90 champion offspring—a record for the breed. Anstamm won the Lloyd Trophy (given to the top winning Scottie each year by the STCA) eight times with seven dogs. (The record for this trophy is ten.) What is particularly noteworthy is the fact that of the eight times the Lloyd Trophy has been won by Anstamm, six of the wins were acquired by owner-handled dogs. No other owner-handlers have won this award since 1969.

Anstamm, now approaching the half century mark, is the oldest active Scottish Terrier kennel in the United States. It maintains that same human-canine relationship that was established between Buffy and "Cimmie" those many years ago.

RICHARD G. BEAUCHAMP

HISTORY and Origin of the Scottish Terrier

The Scottish Terrier, "Scottie," or "Scotsman" as many call the breed, is as spare and reflective of a waste-not, want-not attitude as any MacDougal, MacDonald, or McCandlish as you might ever want to meet. The breed wastes nothing in stature or in character. He is truly a product of his homeland and through the ages has managed to resist most attempts on the part of the misguided who might have had need to transform him into something of their own liking. The story of the Scottish Terrier actually traces back through the centuries to the beginning of time as we know it.

As the mists of the dawn of civilization began to clear, a relationship between man and a beast of the forest had already begun to form. Then man's major pursuits were simply providing food for himself and his family and protecting the members of the tribe from the many dangers that threatened their existence.

Early man undoubtedly saw his own survival efforts reflected in the habits of this beast that made ever increasing overtures at coexistence. That beast was none other than *Canis lupus*–the gray wolf.

The road from wolf in the wild to "man's best friend," *Canis familiaris*, is as long and fascinating as it is fraught with widely varying explanations. However, it seems obvious that observation of the wolf could easily have taught early man some effective hunting skills that he would be able to use advantageously. Wolves saw in man's discards a source of easily secured food. The association grew from there.

The wolves that could assist man in satisfying the unending human need for food were, of course, most highly prized. It also became increasingly obvious as the man-wolf relationship developed through the ages that certain descendants of these increasingly domesticated wolves could also be used by man to assist in survival pursuits other than hunting. Some of these wolves were large enough and strong enough to assist man as a beast of burden. Others were aggressive enough to protect man and the tribe he lived with from danger.

The Arctic or Nordic group of dogs is a direct descendent of the rugged gray wolf (*Canis lupus*). Included in the many breeds of this group are the Alaskan Malamute, Chow Chow, German Shepherd, and more important to the Scottish Terrier, the much smaller Welsh Corgi and Spitz-type dogs. It is thought that the terriers are most probably derived from the small Spitz dogs of the neolithic pile dwellers. From this branch of the Nordic group came small dogs that pursued foxes or badgers into their burrows and were also trained to hunt small vermin.

The Scottish Terrier's heritage lies in the rocky, rugged terrain of Scotland's coastline.

The Northern group, like their undomesticated ancestors,

maintained the characteristics that protect from the harsh environment of the upper European countries. Weather-resistant coats protected from rain and cold. There was a longer coarse outercoat that shed snow and rain and a dense undercoat that insulated against sub-zero temperatures. These coats were often especially abundant around the neck and chest, thereby offering double protection for the vital organs.

Small prick ears were not as easily frostbitten or frozen as the large and pendulous ear of some of the other breeds. The muzzle had sufficient length to warm the frigid air before it reached the lungs. Tails were carried horizontally or up over the back, rather than trailing behind in the snow.

As the species *Homo sapiens* began to harness the abilities of the family Canidae for utilitarian purposes, they crossed a bit of this with a bit of that, and, if the first attempt didn't produce the kind of dog that could and would perform a specific duty, they brought in a dash of something else. In the end they came

The noble Scottish Terrier has an illustrious history, dating back to the late 16th century. Ch. Charthill's Solid Oak.

up with a dog that could get the job done. It goes without saying that the resulting littermates did not always resemble each other closely, nor were they particularly esthetically pleasing, but that was not the point. Later man began to see that dogs constructed in a certain way might be better suited to performing a particular task. Thus form began to follow function. It was the dawning of what we now refer to as "breed type."

These early breeding practices were not an artistic or scientific exercise. They were born of necessity and their implementation was quite elementary. If the dog performed well, it stayed. If it failed the performance test, it went. It was just as simple as that. Consequently, there was little thought given to writing anything down, that is, if the owners of the dogs could write. Either the dog caught the rabbit, pulled the cart, or chased off the intruder, or it didn't. No thought was given to recording the success or failure of these proceedings or to hypothesize reasons for the outcome.

Therefore the actual origin of a breed as old as the Scottish Terrier is somewhat obscure. The more imaginative dog historian usually refers to this obscurity as "a foundation shrouded in mystery." In the case of the Scottie, it is probably due far more to the fact that the Scots were too involved in eking out a living and doing battle with the clan down the road to bother shrouding their somewhat pragmatic breeding programs in mystery.

Today's Scottish Terriers come in a vast array of colors, including gray, brindle, sandy, and wheaten. "Brighton," a brindle colored Scottie, is owned by Charla Hill.

At any rate, most dog writers from the early 1800s on seem to agree that there were two varieties of terriers existing in Britain at the time—a "rough-haired Scotch Terrier" and a "smooth English Terrier."

Thomas Brown, in his *Biographical Sketches and Authentic Anecdotes of Dogs* (1829) said, "The Scotch Terrier is certainly the purest in point of breed and the (smooth) English seems to have been produced by a cross from him." Brown went on to say that the Scotch Terrier was "low in stature, seldom more than 12 or 14 inches in height, with a strong muscular body, and short stout legs." He described the ears as "small" with a "head rather large in proportion to the size of his body." The description went on to say the breed was "generally of a sandy color or black" and that "dogs of these colors are certainly the most hardy, and more to be depended upon." The coat of these dogs is described as "long, matted, and hard, over almost every part of the body."

While the "Scotch Terrier" referred to here was undoubtedly more a generic term than reference to a specific breed, it authenticates the existence of a hard, small, rough-coated terrier developed expressly for work (i.e., hunting small game in the rocky Highlands) as early as several hundred years ago. The description embodies all that is essential to what once was called the "Aberdeen Terrier" and is today's Scottish Terrier.

According to Cindy Cooke's exhaustively researched history of the breed in her book *The New Scottish Terrier*, standardization of breed type or, for that matter, breed name, did not really begin until the late 1800s. The Birmingham, England show of 1860 was the first show to offer classes for Scottish Terriers. At that time, however, seemingly any dog that was "not too large, had some length of coat, a smart expression, and a willingness to kill rats was allowed to compete in the breed classes."

Dogs exhibited at shows in England during the year 1877 were shown as "Skye Terriers." Again, these were a collection of both long- and short-coated dogs and actually included the ancestors of today's Scottish Terrier. Judges at that time were inclined to consider the longer-coated dogs as true "Skye" Terriers. A short time later, when dog show classes were offered by The Kennel

Mr. J. H. Ludlow's Scottish Terrier "Kildee," who closely resembles today's Scottish Terrier, was registered with the Kennel Club in England at the turn of the century.

The standard for the Scottish Terrier in England was accepted in 1880. This photogenic youngster is owned by Linda Terry.

Club in England for "Scotch Terriers," a surprisingly large entry of 15 was drawn. The day's winners were a dog named Tartan of unknown pedigree and a bitch named Splinter II, who was listed as sired by Comus out of Nimble. Through her influential offspring, Splinter was to become known as the matriarch of the modern Scottish Terrier.

While identification as a breed was sought for the Scottish Terrier through the late 1800s, it was known by many different names. It was alternately called the Highland, Cairn, Diehard and, fairly often, the Aberdeen. During this period, a Mr. J. A. Adamson of Aberdeen, Scotland successfully exhibited a number of his dogs. Shown in the days when the Scottish

Terrier still sought breed identity, his dogs became known as "Aberdeen Terriers." Although there never was a breed of dogs known as Aberdeen Terriers, somehow the name clung on for many years.

The first written standard of the breed was drafted by Mr. J. B. Morrison and Mr. D. J. Thomson Gray. It appeared in Vero Shaw's *Illustrated Book of the Dog*. Particular emphasis was placed upon the dog being thick-set, strong, and compact with a short coat that was to be "hard in texture." Weight was set at about 17 pounds and colors "various shades of gray, or grizzle and brindle." (Black was not in vogue as a Scottie color until almost the turn of the century.) Obviously this standard was a giant stride forward in setting both breed type and a specific name for the breed. Interest and activity in the Scottish Terrier as a show dog developed and progressed steadily past the turn of the century, but was heavily curtailed by World War I.

The breed experienced marked advancement throughout the years between World War I and World War II. A. G. Cowley, breeding under the Albourne prefix, and Robert "Bobby" Chapman, using the Heather prefix, are credited for a good part of this progress, as their respective lines produced outstanding show dogs and brilliant producers. The lines assisted the breed's progress both individually and when intelligent crosses were made of the two lines.

THE SCOTSMAN IN AMERICA

Records indicate John Naylor, a Scottish immigrant residing in Mount Forest, Illinois, introduced the first Scottish Terriers to the United States. He showed Tam Glen, Heather, and Bonnie Bell in classes for "Rough-haired Terriers" in 1883. Two years later, Naylor registered the first of the breed with the *National American Kennel Club Stud Book*, the registry source that preceded the American Kennel Club. The dog's name was Prince Charlie and he was listed as being bred in Canada. This leads one to believe that Scotties were an established breed across the northern border before they came to the United States.

It took some time for the breed to catch on in the United States. A club had been organized in 1885 to advance the position of the breed in America, but languished due to lack of real support. After the turn of the century, the Scottish

Terrier's position of respect grew among ardent dog fanciers and the breed was gaining acceptance as a family companion as well.

Assisting the Scottie's quest for acceptance was The Scottish Terrier Club of America, which was organized in 1900 by ardent fancier Dr. Fayette Ewing. Primarily eastern in scope for nearly half a century, the STCA was expanded to include and assist all Scottish Terrier fanciers in the 1950s. To this day, Scottie entries at all-breed dog shows remain moderate, but when a good dog comes along, it is surely a breed to be reckoned with in the show ring.

A true all-American at heart, the first Scottish Terrier was registered in the US in 1884.

Scotties have triumphed at Westminster Kennel Club, America's "show of shows," on at least six occasions—the first when the male Ch. Tickle 'Em Jock scored Best in Show in 1911, and the most recent when the female Ch. Gaelforce Post Script took the top award in 1995.

Without a doubt, the most widely known American-bred Scottish Terrier is Ch. Braeburn's Close Encounter, the breed's all-time top winner with 214 all-breed Bests in Show to her credit. "Shannon" was bred by Ron and Helen Girling and was handled throughout her show career by George Ward. Shannon won her first Best in Show at two years of age and her last at the age of ten.

CHARACTERISTICS of the Scottish Terrier

Before anyone tries to decide whether or not the Scottish Terrier is the correct breed for them, a larger more important question must be asked. That question is "Should I own a dog at all?" Dog ownership is a serious responsibility that is time consuming and should not be entered into lightly. Failure to understand this can make what can be a rewarding relationship one of sheer drudgery. This is also one of the primary reasons for thousands upon thousands of unwanted dogs ending their lives in humane societies and animal shelters throughout America.

If the prospective dog owner lives alone, all he or she needs do is be sure that there is a strong desire to make the necessary commitment dog ownership entails. In the case of family households, it is vital that the person who will ultimately be responsible for the dog's care really wants a dog. In the average household, mothers are most often given the additional responsibility of caring for the family pets, although today they too are out in the workplace. All too often it is the mother who is saddled with the additional chores of feeding and trips to the veterinary hospital with what was supposed to be a family project.

Who knows how far your Scottie will go? Three-and-one-half-week-old "Tigger" will grow up to be Ch. Blairesk's Bengal Legend.

Nearly all children love puppies and dogs and will promise anything to get one. But childhood enthusiasm can wane very quickly and it will be up to the adults in the family to ensure that the dog

The active and inquisitive Scottish Terrier is no stranger to mischief!

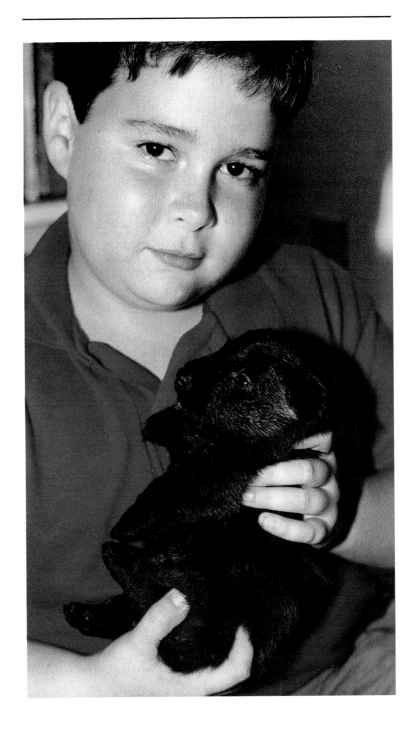

receives proper care. Children should be taught responsibility, but to expect a living, breathing, and needy animal to teach a child this lesson is incredibly indifferent to the needs of the animal.

There are many households in which the entire family is gone from early morning until late in the day. The question that must be asked here is "Who will provide food for the dog and access to the outdoors so that he can relieve himself?" This is something that can probably be worked out with an adult dog, but it is totally unfair for anyone to expect a young puppy to survive these conditions.

Should an individual or family find they are capable of providing the proper home for a dog or young puppy, suitability of breed must also be considered. It might be worthwhile to look at the difference between owning a purebred dog and one of mixed ancestry.

A mongrel can give you as much love and devotion as a purebred dog. However, the manner in which the dog does this and how his personality, energy level, and the amount of care he requires suits an individual's lifestyle are major considerations. In a purebred dog, most of these considerations are predictable to a marked degree, even if the dog is purchased as a very young puppy. A puppy of uncertain parentage will not give you this assurance.

All puppies are cute and fairly manageable, but someone who lives in a two-room apartment will find life difficult with a dog that grows to the size of a Great Dane. The mountain

A puppy may be irresistible, but be certain to educate yourself about the responsibilities of owning a dog before you bring one home.

20

climber or marathon runner is not going to be happy with a short-nosed breed that has difficulty catching his breath from simply walking across the street on a hot day.

An owner who expects his or her dog to sit quietly while he watches television or reads is not going to be particularly happy with a high-strung, off-the-wall dog whose

Personalities vary among puppies, so be sure to choose one that will fit with your lifestyle.

The Scottish Terrier's loving and happy disposition makes him a welcome addition to most families.

rest requirements are 30 seconds out of every 10 hours. Nor is the outdoorsman going to be particularly happy with a long-coated breed that attracts every burr, leaf, and insect in all of nature. Knowing what kind of dog best suits your lifestyle is not just a consideration—it is paramount to the foundation of your life-long relationship with the dog.

LIFE WITH A SCOTTIE

While evaluation in the show ring is undoubtedly our best guide to assessing the external virtues of the Scottish Terrier, in reality that is actually secondary in the list of characteristics that affect the pet Scottie owner most. Sound temperament ranks first and foremost with the owner of a Scottie in the home. By and large, dedicated and responsible Scottie breeders have been loyal to the breed's original character and purpose.

As appealing as the jaunty tailored look of the breed may be, devotees of the breed develop this loyalty not because of the breed's looks, but because of the breed's distinctive character. Although Scotties want to be loved, they will only do so much to please you, and then usually when they see fit and only in the manner they consider appropriate.

Dedicated Scottie breeders are careful to be true to the breed's original character and purpose.

This is not to say the Scottie is insensitive. On the contrary, when verbally chastened for some misdeed, a Scottie will lower his ears, duck his head, and creep off to a corner in disgrace to nurse wounded feelings.

Scottie owners are inclined to believe this reaction is due in part to having been scolded but also in disbelief that anyone would think there was malice aforethought in their behavior. "Doesn't my owner know I had good reason to do what I did?"

Recognizing the fact that the Scottie's nature appeals to a very particular kind of person, sincere breeders have made little attempt to make the breed a popular one. This limited appeal is not unlike the Scottie's own discerning taste in humans.

While there may be an occasional Scottie that assigns himself the duties of household "welcome wagon," one is far more apt to find the breed reserved and dignified in the presence of those who are not members of his immediate household. While the Scottie is entirely devoted to his

Although the Scottie is generally considered to be reserved at first, once you win his affection he will become very attached to his loved ones.

master or mistress and is more than happy to extend that devotion to his loved one's immediate family, strangers are an entirely different matter. A Scottie has to make that decision on an individual basis. Discerning? A perfect word to describe this unique breed!

Gardening enthusiasts and people who take inordinate pride in their perfectly maintained lawns should be forewarned that Scotties are unsurpassed as excavators. One of their primary missions in life is to seek out and destroy ground vermin wherever they may (or may not) exist!

A Scottie has big paws and big teeth and uses them both quickly and effectively for excavating and for turning things loose from their moorings. A growing Scottie is determined to see all objects, animate and otherwise, free from restrictions, so a part of his day might well be spent freeing your lamp from its cord, a leg from its chair, food staples from their cupboards, or himself from his leash.

The difficulty some might experience with a Scottie is that in most cases he will be firmly convinced that what he has done is something that an ounce of sense would tell you should have been done. The Scottish Terrier is no less difficult to dissuade than the Scots who created the breed in the first place.

Don't think for a moment that because of his determined nature that the Scottie is humorless. Not so! This is one of the most endearing qualities of the breed. The Scottie can amuse himself for hours on end and will do everything in his power to invent things to elicit a chuckle, even a belly-laugh, from his owner.

Your Scottie will love and adore you, but don't expect him to lavish this affection on you. With Scottish reserve, your dog will let you know just how important you are to his existence and how much he missed you while you were gone. But you will know full well he is sincere and not for the world at large—only you.

The Scottie is not a barker, but will always let you know when he suspects something is not as it should be. It is a breed that is outrageously independent and incredibly courageous. While the breed is never one to go out of his way to pick a fight, he is ready, willing, and able to defend himself, his family, or his territory. The Scottie has earned his nickname "the Diehard" quite legitimately.

Like any Scottie, Ch. Hycourt's Blessed Assurance is dedicated to ridding his yard of vermin!

MALE OR FEMALE?

While the sex of a dog in many breeds is a very important consideration, this is not particularly the case with the Scottie. The male Scottie makes just as loving, devoted, and trainable a companion as the female. In fact, there are some that believe that a male can be even more devoted to his master than female.

Whether male or female, the Scottie will make an equally loving, devoted, and trainable companion.

There is one important point to consider in determining your choice between male and female. While both must be trained not to relieve themselves just anywhere in the home, males have a natural instinct to lift their leg and urinate to "mark" their home territory. It seems confusing to many dog owners, but a male marking his home turf has absolutely nothing to do with whether or not he is housebroken. The two responses come from entirely different needs and must be dealt with in that manner. Some dogs are more difficult to train not to mark within the confines of the household than others. Males that are used for breeding are even more prone to this response and are even harder to break of the habit.

On the other hand, females have their semiannual "heat" cycles once they have reached sexual maturity. In the case of the female Scottie, this can occur for the first time at about nine or ten months of age and the cycle lasts approximately three weeks. These cycles are accompanied by a vaginal discharge, so it is important to keep the female off furniture or carpeting that can be stained. Special pants can be used to avoid this soiling. It must be understood, however, that the female has no control over this bloody discharge, so it has nothing to do with training.

While Scotties are not normally left outdoors unattended for long stretches of time, this is one time a female should not be outdoors by herself for even a brief moment or two. The need for confinement of the female in heat is especially important to prevent her becoming pregnant by some neighborhood Lothario.

Both the male's and female's sexually related problems can usually be eliminated by spaying the female and neutering the male. Unless a Scottie has been purchased expressly for breeding or showing from a breeder capable of making this judgment, your dog should be sexually altered.

The Scottish Terrier has a number of unique qualities that make him a versatile and amiable breed.

Breeding and raising puppies should be left in the hands of people who have the facilities to keep each and every puppy they breed until the correct home is found for it. This can often take many months after a litter is born, a job for which most single dog owners are not equipped.

Naturally, a responsible Scottie owner would never allow his or her pet to roam the streets and end his life in an animal shelter. Unfortunately, being forced to place a puppy due to space constraints before you are able to thoroughly check out the prospective buyer may in fact create this exact situation. Today, most respected breeders require that all pet-quality puppies they sell be spayed or neutered.

Many times parents ask to buy a female "just as a pet" but with full intentions of breeding so that their children can witness the birth process. There are countless books and videos now available that portray this wonderful event and do not add to the worldwide pet overpopulation we now face. Altering one's companion dogs not only precludes the possibility of adding to this problem; it also eliminates bothersome household problems and precautions.

It should be understood, however, that spaying and neutering are not reversible procedures. Spayed females or neutered males are not allowed to be shown in conformation shows, nor will altered animals ever be able to be used for breeding.

This adorable three-week-old Scottie puppy bred by Lois Bolding is a perfect example of good breeding.

STANDARD for the Scottish Terrier

The American Kennel Club standard for the Scottish Terrier is written in simple straightforward language that can be read and understood by even the beginning fancier. What it implies, however, takes many years to fully understand. This can only be accomplished through observing many quality Scotties over the years and reading as much about the breed as possible. Many books have been written about the breed and it is well worth the Scottie owner's time and

The Scottish Terrier has a pleasing expression—intelligent, alert, soft, and appealing.

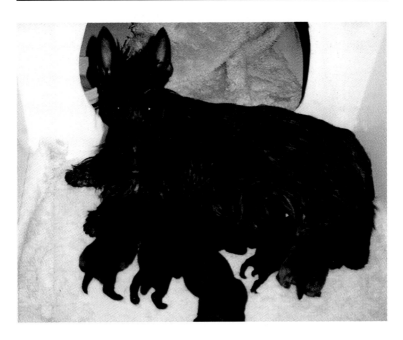

A well-bred Scottish Terrier pup can be anything you desire—a champion, a companion, a therapy dog, and more—but definitely a best friend!

effort to digest their contents if he or she is interested in showing or breeding.

There are some breeds that change drastically from puppyhood to adulthood. It would be extremely difficult for the untrained eye to determine the actual breed of some purebred dogs in puppyhood. This is not so with the Scottie. In many respects, at eight weeks of age a Scottie puppy will reflect in miniature what it will look like at maturity.

It must be remembered that a breed standard describes the "ideal" Scottie, but no dog is perfect and no dog, not even the greatest dog show winner, will possess every quality asked for in its perfect form. It is how closely an individual dog adheres to the standard of the breed that determines his show potential.

One of the things that makes the Scottie such an attractive dog is that, even though he is not particularly large, he is a very substantial dog. He is easily managed, but far from fragile in any respect. Everything about the quality Scottie denotes rugged power and independence. Although in this day and age the Scottie is entirely dependent upon his owner for all his needs, you will have trouble convincing any true member of the breed this is so. The Scottie lives with you as a partner and though you may provide food and shelter, he sees this simply as your contribution to the partnership.

OFFICIAL STANDARD FOR THE SCOTTISH TERRIER

General Appearance—The Scottish Terrier is a small, compact, short-legged, sturdily-built dog of good bone and substance. His head is long in proportion to his size. He has a hard, wiry, weather-resistant coat and a thick-set, cobby body which is hung between short, heavy legs. These characteristics, joined with his very special keen, piercing, "varminty" expression, and his erect ears and tail are salient features of the breed. The Scottish Terrier's bold, confident, dignified aspect exemplifies power in a small package.

Size, Proportion and Substance—The Scottish Terrier should have a thick body and heavy bone. The principle objective must be symmetry and balance without exaggeration. Equal consideration shall be given to height, weight, length of back and length of head. Height at withers for either sex should be about 10 inches. The length of back from withers to set-on of tail should be approximately 11 inches. Generally, a well-balanced Scottish Terrier dog should weigh from 19 to 22 pounds and a bitch from 18 to 21 pounds.

Head—The head should be long in proportion to the overall length and size of the dog. In profile, the skull and muzzle

should give the appearance of two parallel planes. The *skull* should be long and of medium width, slightly domed and covered with short, hard hair. In profile, the skull should appear flat. There should be a

The head of the Scottish Terrier should be clean cut, long, and of medium width. Ch. Boldmere Tarred 'n Feathered owned by Mary Dyer.

30

slight but definite stop between the skull and muzzle at eye level, allowing the eyes to set in under the brow, contributing to proper Scottish Terrier expression. The skull should be smooth with no prominences or depressions and the cheeks should be flat and clean. The *muzzle* should be approximately equal to the length of skull with only a slight taper to the nose. The muzzle should be well filled in under the eye, with no evidence of snipeyness. A correct Scottish Terrier muzzle should fill an average's man's hand. The *nose* should be black, regardless of coat color, and of good size, projecting

Ch. Braeburn's Close Encounter is the greatest winning Scottish Terrier of all time, winning over 200 all-breed Best in Show awards. She was bred by Ron and Helen Girling and handled by George Ward.

The neck of the Scottie should be strong, short, thick, and muscular, blending smoothly into the shoulders.

somewhat over the mouth and giving the impression that the upper jaw is longer than the lower. The *teeth* should be large and evenly spaced, having either a scissor or level bite, the former preferred. The jaw should be square, level and powerful. Undershot or overshot bites should be penalized. The *eyes* should be set wide apart and well in under the brow. They should be small, bright and piercing, and almond-shaped, not round. The color should be dark brown or nearly black, the darker the better. The *ears* should be small, prick, set well up on the skull and pointed, but never cut. They should be covered with short velvety hair. From the front, the outer edge of the ear should form a straight line up from the side of the skull. The use, size, shape and placement of the ear and its erect carriage are major elements of the keen, alert, intelligent Scottish Terrier expression.

The Scottish Terrier's coat should be hard and wiry to the touch, with a soft, dense undercoat.

Neck, Topline, Body—The *neck* should be moderately short, strong, thick and muscular, blending smoothly into well laid back shoulders. The neck must never be so short as to appear clumsy. The *body* should be moderately short with ribs extending well back into a short, strong loin, deep flanks and very muscular hindquarters. The ribs should be well sprung out from the spine, forming a broad, strong back, then curving down and inward to form a deep body that would be nearly heart-shaped if viewed in cross-section. The *topline* of the back should be firm and level. The *chest* should be broad, very deep, and well let down between the forelegs. The forechest should extend well in front of the legs and drop well down into the brisket. The chest should not be flat or concave, and the brisket should nicely fill an average man's slightly cupped hand. The lowest point of the brisket should be such that an average man's fist would fit under it with little or no overhead clearance. The *tail* should be about seven

The overall appearance of the Scottish Terrier should be bold, confident, and dignified power wrapped up in a small package.

inches long and never cut. It should be set on high and carried erectly, either vertical or with a slight curve forward, but not over the back. The tail should be thick at the base, tapering gradually to a point and covered with short, hard hair.

Forequarters—The shoulders should be well laid back and moderately well knit at the withers. The forelegs should be very heavy in bone, straight or slightly bent with elbows close to the body, and set in under the shoulder blade with a definite forechest in front of them.

The ears of a Scottie will stand erect naturally by the age of four months.

Scottish Terriers should not be out at the elbows. The *forefeet* should be larger than the hind feet, round, thick, and compact with strong nails. The front feet should point straight ahead, but a slight "toeing out" is acceptable. Dew claws may be removed.

Hindquarters—The thighs should be very muscular and powerful for the size of the dog with the stifles well bent and the legs straight from back to heel. Hocks should be well let down and parallel to each other.

Coat—The Scottish Terrier should have a broken coat. It is a hard, wiry outer coat with a soft, dense undercoat. The coat should be trimmed and blended into the furnishings to give a distinct Scottish Terrier outline. The dog should be presented with sufficient coat so that the texture and density may be determined. The longer coat on the beard, legs and lower body may be slightly softer than the body coat but should not appear fluffy.

Color—Black, wheaten or brindle of any color. Many black and brindle dogs have sparklings of white or silver hairs in their coats which are normal and not to be penalized. White can be allowed only on the chest and chin and that to a slight extent only.

Gait—The gait of the Scottish Terrier is very characteristic of the breed. It is not the square trot or walk

The coat of the Scottish Terrier may be black, brindle, or wheaten in color.

desirable in the long-legged breeds. The forelegs do not move in exact parallel planes; rather, in reaching out, the forelegs incline slightly inward because of the deep broad forechest. Movement should be free, agile, and coordinated with powerful drive from the rear and good reach in front. The action of the rear legs should be square and true and, at the trot, both the hocks and stifles should be flexed with a vigorous motion. When the dog is in motion, the back should remain firm and level.

Temperament—The Scottish Terrier should be alert and spirited but also stable and steady-going. He is a determined and thoughtful dog whose "heads up, tails up" attitude in the ring should convey both fire and control. The Scottish Terrier, while loving and gentle with people, can be aggressive with other dogs. He should exude ruggedness and power, living up to his nickname, the "Diehard."

Penalties—Soft coat; curly coat; round,

The alert and spirited temperament of a Scottie should be apparent from puppyhood.

The Scottish Terrier's tail should be set on high and carried erectly.

protruding, or light eyes; overshort or undershot jaws; obviously oversize or undersize; shyness or timidity; upright shoulders; lack of reach in front or drive in rear; stiff or stilted movement; movement too wide or too close in rear; too narrow in front or rear; out at the elbow; lack of bone and substance; low set tail; lack of pigment in the nose; coarse head; and failure to show head and tail up are faults to be penalized.

NO JUDGE SHOULD PUT TO WINNERS OR BEST OF BREED ANY SCOTTISH TERRIER NOT SHOWING REAL TERRIER CHARACTER IN THE RING.

Scale of Points

Skull	5
Muzzle	5
Eyes	5
Ears	10
Neck	5
Chest	5
Body	15
Legs & Feet	10
Tail	5
Coat	15
Size	10
General Appearance	10
Total	100

SELECTING the Right Scottish Terrier for You

WHERE TO BUY YOUR SCOTTIE

The Scottie you buy will live with you for many years to come. It is not the least bit unusual for the well-bred Scottie to live as long as 12 or even 14 years of age. Obviously, it is important that the Scottie you select has the advantage of beginning life in a healthy environment and comes from sound, healthy stock.

The only way you can be sure of this is to go directly to a breeder who has earned a reputation over the years for consistently producing Scotties that are mentally and physically sound. The way a breeder is able to earn this reputation is through a well-planned breeding program that has been governed by rigid selectivity. Selective breeding programs are aimed at maintaining the breed's many fine qualities and eliminating any genetic weaknesses.

Your Scottish Terrier will have a good start in life if his parents are happy and well adjusted. Make sure to see the dam and sire of the puppy you are considering.

This process is both time consuming and costly for a breeder, but it ensures you of getting a dog that will be a joy to own. Responsible Scottie breeders protect their investment by basing their breeding programs on the healthiest, most representative stock available and providing each succeeding generation with the very best care and nutrition.

The governing kennel clubs in the different countries of the world maintain lists of local breed clubs and breeders that can lead a prospective Scottie buyer to responsible breeders of quality stock. If you are not sure of where to contact an established Scottish Terrier breeder in your area, we strongly suggest contacting your local kennel club for recommendations.

It is highly likely that you will be able to find an established Scottie breeder in your own area. If so, you will be able to visit the breeder, inspect the premises, and in many cases, you will also be able to see a puppy's parents and other relatives. These

breeders are always willing and able to discuss any problems that exist in the breed and how they should be dealt with.

Should there be no breeders in your immediate area, you can arrange to have a puppy shipped to you. There are many established breeders throughout the country that have shipped puppies to satisfied owners out of state and even to other countries.

Never hesitate to ask the breeder you visit any questions or concerns you might have relating to Scottie ownership. You should expect the breeder to ask you a good number of questions as well. Good breeders are just as interested in placing their puppies in a loving and safe environment as you are in obtaining a happy, healthy puppy.

Be sure to do your homework and learn all you can about the breed before making the decision to bring a Scottish Terrier into your home.

A breeder will undoubtedly want to know if there are young children in the family and if you or your children have ever owned a dog before. The breeder will want to know if you have a yard with a real fence. Electronic fences simply do not work with Scotties! Will someone be home during the day to attend to a young puppy's needs? If there is a pond or pool on the

premises, is there adequate fencing to keep your Scottie safely away from it? Scotties are notoriously poor swimmers and what little ability they might have in that area is completely lost as they panic to get out of water in which they have fallen. If you get an in-depth interrogation from a breeder you can feel fairly confident you have found one that truly cares about where his or her dogs will be living.

Registration papers will prove that the parents of your puppy were purebred Scottish Terriers.

Not all good breeders maintain large kennels. In fact, you are more apt to find that many Scotties come from the homes of small hobby breeders who keep only a few dogs and have litters only occasionally. The names of these people are just as likely to appear on the recommended lists from kennel clubs as the larger kennels that maintain many dogs. Hobby breeders are equally dedicated to breeding quality Scotties and have the distinct advantage of being able to raise their puppies in the home environment with all the accompanying personal attention and socialization.

Needless to say, cleanliness is the bottom line when it comes to raising dogs of any breed. Puppies should always be kept in a warm lighted area and the adult dogs should be maintained in an equally pleasant and sanitary area.

A breeder's membership in at least one Scottish Terrier Club can tell the prospective buyer a great deal about the person's desire to learn and to live up to certain standards of quality. If the breeder is not a club member, the recommendation of the person by someone who is a club member can be valuable, and breeders who show their dogs indicate a desire on their part to maintain a high standard of quality.

Again, it is important that both the buyer and the seller ask questions. After all, this is an adoption process, not a business deal. A buyer should be highly suspect of a person who is willing to sell you a Scottie puppy with no questions asked.

BREED PROBLEMS

Our discussion of hereditary health problems in Scotties must be prefaced with the fact that all breeds of dogs have health concerns—even mongrels. Scotties are no exception, but this does not mean all Scotties are afflicted by even one of the following. This is why a search for honest responsible breeders is so important. Should the breeder you are speaking to be unaware of these breed problems our advice is to leave without a dog—immediately!

Scottie Cramp

This is not actually a cramp as such, but is thought to be the result of a deficiency of serotonin that causes locomotion problems when the dog is under heavy stress or after heavy exercise. It has been observed in young puppies as well as adults. This is not normally a problem for the average house pet in that he is seldom put under the kind of strain that initiates the condition. It appears that afflicted dogs sometimes anticipate the onset of the cramping and are often able to adjust their activity to compensate. When stress or activity is removed, the afflicted dog returns to normal. Treatment is seldom necessary.

Epilepsy

Fortunately, epilepsy is not rampant in the breed, but there have been enough cases reported to warrant cautioning the buyer to discuss the problem with a prospective breeder. The epileptic Scottie will have recurring seizures that may or may not cause unconsciousness. There is a stiffening of the limbs and usually the dog in seizure will salivate heavily. There is no known cause for this hereditary problem, but any dog that has a seizure should be taken to a veterinarian at once.

Cranial Mandibular Osteopathy

This is an abnormal growth in the jawbone of puppies. It is evidenced by extreme sensitivity in the mouth and head area. Afflicted puppies are extremely sensitive to being touched in those areas and will recoil in extreme pain. It can be treated and it is often outgrown.

Last one out is a rotten Scottie! Playfulness and activity are often signs of a healthy and well-adjusted puppy.

Von Willebrand's Disease

This is similar in many respects to hemophilia but the bleeding, while excessive, is less severe than a hemophiliac would experience. Bleeding can be internal.

Responsible breeders will not sell a puppy that is afflicted and if a breeder appears to be unfamiliar with the disease, you should not consider buying a puppy from him.

RECOGNIZING A HEALTHY PUPPY

Most breeders do not release their puppies to their new homes before the puppies are 12 to 14 weeks of age and have been given most of their puppy inoculations. By the time the litter is eight weeks of age, they are entirely weaned and no longer nursing on their mother.

While the puppies were nursing, they had a certain degree of immunity from their mother. This immunity is acquired from the colostrum, which is the milk produced by the mother

Encourage your puppy to explore the world around him. New experiences will enrich his life. These junior explorers were bred by Lois Bolding.

in the first 24-36 hours after whelping. The length of time this immunity exists varies and depends entirely upon the degree of immunity of the female. Therefore, breeders are extremely protective of young puppies until the puppies have been vaccinated.

Puppies are highly susceptible to many infectious diseases until they have been inoculated. A number of these diseases can be transmitted on the hands and clothing of humans. Therefore, it is extremely important that all puppies are kept current on all the shots they must have for their age.

SELECTING A PUPPY

A healthy Scottie puppy is a bouncy, playful extrovert. Never select a puppy that appears shy or listless because you feel sorry for him. Doing so will undoubtedly lead to heartache and expensive veterinary costs. Do not attempt to make up for what the breeder did not do in providing proper care and nutrition. It seldom works.

Scottie puppies can be indifferent to strangers, but they should not be shy or fearful. It is not entirely untypical for a Scottie puppy to ignore the buyer who tries to get him to come running over. The same puppy may not be particularly pleased about being held by a stranger and may squirm to get down.

If at all possible, take the puppy you are attracted to into a different room in the kennel or house. The smells will remain the same for the puppy, so he should still feel secure and it will give you an opportunity to inspect the puppy more closely and see how he acts away from his littermates.

Size is relatively unimportant in terms of health. A puppy that is smaller or larger than his littermates or over or under standard size can still make a perfectly good pet.

Well-cared-for puppies are plump and content right from birth. Responsible breeders take great pains to ensure the health of their breeding stock.

Scottie puppies should feel sturdy to the touch. They should not feel bony, nor should their abdomens be bloated or extended. A puppy that has just eaten may have a belly that is full, but the puppy should never appear obese.

A healthy puppy's ears will be pink and clean. Dark discharge or a bad odor could indicate ear mites, a sure sign of lack of cleanliness and poor maintenance. A Scottie puppy's breath should always smell sweet. His teeth must be clean and bright, and there should never be a malformation of the jaw, lips, or nostrils.

Scottie eyes are dark and clear. Runny eyes or eyes that appear red and irritated could be caused by a myriad of problems, none of which indicate a healthy puppy.

Coughing or diarrhea are danger signals, as is any discharge from the nose or eruptions on the skin. Note the skin and coat condition of the puppy's parents if they are available. Skin and coat problems can be hereditary. The puppy's coat should be clean and healthy looking. Needless to say, there should be no fleas or parasites of any kind in the coat.

The puppy's attitude tells you a great deal about his state of health. Puppies that are feeling "out of sorts" react very quickly, will usually find a warm littermate to snuggle up to, and will prefer to stay that way even when the rest of the "gang" wants to play or go exploring.

The Scottie puppy is an independent and self-assured little tyke. Those who anticipate the purchase of a Scottie should never settle for anything less than a specimen that truly represents the breed, in both ruggedness of appearance and determined character. While we don't expect the Scottie to go to battle for us and it may never have to rout a rodent from the kitchen or a fox from the hen house, the instinct to do so should be there. Do not settle for anything less in selecting your puppy.

SELECTING A SHOW-PROSPECT PUPPY

There is a color range from which to choose your Scottie. The breed standard allows "black, wheaten or brindle of any color," but color has no bearing on the Scottie's character, and, if the show ring is your ultimate aim, "a good dog, like a good horse, cannot be a bad color."

While the fluffy Scottie pup may be cute, if you want the correct hard-coated adult, bypass the fluffy one and go for the smoother youngster with less furnishings. He or she will undoubtedly grow up with the easiest coat to care for.

The Scottie puppy should always be short coupled and sturdy with a low center of gravity. The puppy is not easily bowled over and should give the impression of being totally in command of the ground he stands on.

The Scottie's head is long and his back is moderately short. The tail is carried boldly erect and the dark eyes

When searching for a Scottish Terrier puppy, do as much research as possible and avoid making a hasty decision. This Springbok Kennels pup takes a break amongst the Texas bluebonnets.

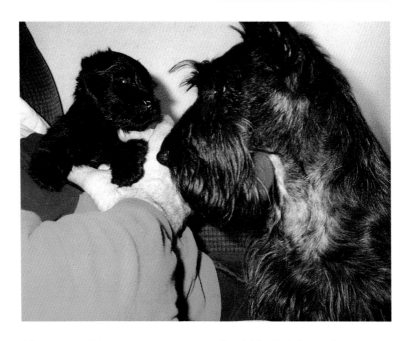

There is nothing quite as endearing as the relationship between a mother and her young. However, keep in mind that taking care of a litter of puppies means a lot of time and work for you.

should be bright and piercing. His alert expression is enhanced by neat pointed ears. Scottie ears stand naturally and normally do so by the time the pup is three months old.

If you or your family are considering a show career for your puppy, we strongly advise putting yourself in the hands of an established breeder who has not only earned a reputation for breeding winning show dogs, but who is also willing to assist the novice. Look for a breeder who is capable of giving an honest evaluation of his or her show prospects. Be wary of a breeder who has entire litters of "show prospects." Show-quality puppies simply do not appear that frequently.

Although the potential buyer should read the American Kennel Club Standard of Perfection for the Scottish Terrier, it is hard for the novice to really understand the nuances of what is being asked. The experienced breeder is best equipped to do so and will be only too happy to assist you in your quest.

Even at that, no one can make accurate predictions or guarantees on a very young puppy, and most established Scottie breeders keep their show prospect puppies until they are at least six to seven months old before they are willing to predict a successful show career with any degree of certainty.

By this age, the breeder will have done initial trimming on the puppy and will undoubtedly have taken him to several match shows or training classes so that the puppy will be leash trained. When a puppy has learned to walk calmly on the leash, it will be considerably easier to evaluate how well he moves.

Any predictions a breeder is apt to make are based upon the breeder's experience with past litters that produced winning show dogs. It should be obvious that the more successful a breeder has been in producing winning Scotties through the years, the broader his or her basis of comparison will be.

The most any responsible breeder will say about an eight-week-old puppy is that he has "promise." If you are serious about showing your Scottie, most reliable breeders strongly suggest waiting until a puppy is over six months old before making any decisions. If the puppy you select is of this age or older, many breeders are willing to guarantee the puppy's suitability for the show ring in writing.

There are many "beauty point" shortcomings a Scottie puppy might have that would in no way interfere with his being a wonderful companion, but these faults would be serious drawbacks in the show ring. Many of these flaws are

The Scottish Terrier puppy you choose should be bright-eyed, healthy, and interested in the world around him.

such that a beginner in the breed would hardly notice. This is why employing the assistance of a good breeder is so important.

All of the foregoing regarding soundness and health applies to the show puppy as well as to the pet puppy. The show prospect must be sound, healthy, and adhere to the standard of the breed very closely.

The complete standard of the breed is printed in this book and it can assist the newcomer in learning more about the show-quality Scottie. The more you know about the history and origin of the breed, the

He may be tiny now, but a Scottish Terrier puppy will attain most of his adult size by six months of age.

better equipped you will be to see the differences that distinguish the show dog from the pet.

Like mother, like daughter! Often, the temperament of a puppy will be much like her parents.

When choosing a show-prospect puppy, look for a confident attitude, overall balance and outline, head

444

qualities, and correct construction. Bone, substance, and movement are things that are considered more seriously as the puppy matures.

PUPPY OR ADULT?

For the person anticipating a show career for their Scottie or for someone hoping to become a breeder, the purchase of a young adult provides greater certainty in respect to quality. Even those who simply want a companion could consider the adult dog.

In some instances, breeders will have males or females for sale that they no longer wish to use for breeding. After the dogs have been altered, the breeder may prefer to have the dogs live out their lives in a private home with attendant care and affection. In other cases, there may be adult Scotties who have lost their home due to the illness or death of their previous owner. In many cities there are Scottie Rescue Services that seek homes for these happy healthy dogs.

Acquiring an adult dog eliminates the many problems raising a puppy involves, and often elderly people prefer the adult dog, particularly one that is housebroken. An adult Scottie is usually far easier to manage, requiring less supervision and damage control. Adult Scotties are also less apt to be "chewers" and have passed through those many exasperating puppy antics.

There are things to consider, though. Adult dogs have usually developed behaviors that may or may not fit into your routine. If a Scottie has never been exposed to small children, the dog may be totally perplexed and often frightened by this new experience. Children are also inclined to be more active and vocal than the average adult and this could intimidate the dog as well.

We strongly advise taking an adult Scottie on a trial basis to see if the dog will adapt to the new owner's lifestyle and environment. Most often it works but, on occasion, a prospective owner decides training his or her dog from puppyhood is worth the time and effort it requires.

IMPORTANT PAPERS

The purchase of any purebred dog entitles you to three very important documents: a health record that also includes an inoculation record, a copy of the dog's pedigree, and the registration certificate.

You will find most reputable Scottie breeders have initiated the necessary preliminary inoculation series for their puppies by the time they are six weeks of age. These inoculations temporarily protect the puppies against hepatitis, leptospirosis, distemper, and canine parvovirus. "Permanent" inoculations will follow at a prescribed time. Because different breeders and veterinarians follow different approaches to inoculations, it is important that the health record you obtain for your puppy accurately lists what shots have been given and when. In this way the veterinarian you choose will be able to continue with the appropriate inoculation series as needed. In most cases, rabies inoculations are not given until a puppy is six months of age or older.

The pedigree is your dog's "family tree." The breeder must supply you with a copy of this document authenticating your puppy's ancestors back to at least the third generation. It should be understood that all purebred and registerable dogs have a pedigree. This is no indication that the

Your Scottish Terrier's pedigree will offer you important information about his ancestry.

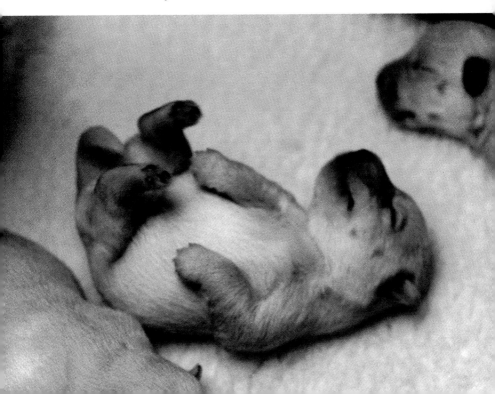

resulting puppy or puppies are of superior or show quality. The pedigree is simply documentation of the fact that all the dogs appearing on the pedigree certificate of your Scottie are purebred.

The registration certificate is the canine world's "birth certificate." This certificate is issued by a country's governing kennel club. When you transfer the ownership of your Scottie from the breeder's name to your own name, the transaction is entered on this certificate and mailed to the appropriate kennel club, and it is permanently recorded in their computerized files.

Keep all of your dog's documents in a safe place as you will need them when you visit your veterinarian or should you ever wish to breed or show your Scottie. Keep the name, address, and phone number of the breeder from whom you purchase your Scottie in a separate place as well. Should you ever lose any of these important documents, you will then be able to contact the breeder in regard to obtaining duplicates.

DIET SHEET

Your Scottie puppy is the happy healthy puppy he is because the breeder has been carefully feeding and caring for him. Every responsible breeder has his or her own particular way of doing this. Most breeders give the new owner a written record that details the amount and kind of food a puppy has been receiving. Follow these recommendations to the letter, at least for the first month or two after the puppy comes to live with you.

The diet sheet should indicate the number of times a day your Scottie has been accustomed to being fed and the kind of

 vitamin supplementation, if any, he has been

Your Scottie will soon "grow into" an adult diet, but during his first few weeks at your home stick to your breeder's recommendation.

receiving. Following the prescribed procedure will reduce the chance of upset stomach and loose stools.

Usually a breeder's diet sheet projects the increases and changes in food that will be necessary as your puppy grows from week to week. If the sheet does not include this information, ask the breeder for suggestions regarding increases and the eventual changeover to adult food.

Upon selection of your Scottish Terrier puppy, the breeder should offer a guarantee against inherited disorders.

In the unlikely event you are not supplied with a diet sheet by the breeder and are unable to get one, your veterinarian will be able to advise you in this respect. There are countless foods now being manufactured expressly to meet the nutritional needs of puppies and growing dogs. A trip down the pet aisle at your supermarket will prove just how many choices you have. Two important tips to remember: read labels carefully for content and when dealing with established reliable manufacturers, you are more likely to get what you pay for.

HEALTH GUARANTEE

A reputable breeder will be more than willing to supply a written agreement stating that the purchase of your Scottie is contingent upon his passing a veterinarian's examination and that he is of sound temperament. Ideally, you will be able to arrange an appointment with your chosen veterinarian right after you have picked up your puppy from the breeder and before you take the puppy home. If this is not possible, you should not delay this procedure any longer than 24 hours from the time you take your puppy home.

TEMPERAMENT AND SOCIALIZATION

Temperament is the result of both heredity and environment. Inherited good temperament can be ruined by poor treatment and lack of proper socialization. A Scottie puppy that comes from shy or nervous stock or exhibits those characteristics will make a poor companion or show dog and should certainly never be bred. Therefore, it is critical that you obtain a happy puppy from a breeder who is determined to produce good temperament and has taken all the necessary steps to provide the early socialization necessary.

Temperaments in the same litter can range from confident and outgoing on the high end of the scale to shy and fearful at the low end. By and large, when intelligently bred, Scottie temperament is and should be sound and reliable. Scottie temperament should be as sturdy as the breed's physique.

Puppyhood is the easiest age to socialize and train your Scottish Terrier.

If you are fortunate enough to have children in the household or living nearby, your socialization task will be assisted considerably. Scotties raised with well-supervised children are the best. The two seem to understand each other and in some way known only to the puppies and children themselves, give each other the confidence to face the trying ordeal of growing up.

The children in your own household are not the only children with whom your Scottie should spend time. It is a case of the more the merrier! Every child (and adult for that matter) that enters your household should be introduced to your Scottie.

Your puppy should go everywhere with you–the post office, the market, the shopping mall–wherever. Be prepared to create a stir wherever you go because the very reason that attracted you to the first Scottie you met applies to other people as well. Everyone will want to pet your little Scotsman and there is nothing in the world better for him. Most Scotties tolerate the attention with a somewhat resigned air, but the interaction is wonderful for the dog.

If your Scottie has a show career in his future, there are other things in

Your Scottish Terrier will look to you, his owner, to take care of his needs.

addition to just being handled that will have to be taught. All show dogs must learn to have their mouths inspected by the judge. The judge must also be able to check the teeth. Males must be accustomed to having their testicles touched, as the dog show judge must determine that all male dogs are "complete," which means there are two normal sized testicles in the scrotum. These inspections must begin in puppyhood and be done on a regular and continuing basis.

THE ADOLESCENT SCOTTISH TERRIER

Scotties attain their full height fairly quickly. Usually by 10 or 11 months of age, a Scottie has grown as tall as he will be, but at that age, the breed is far from mature. Some lines achieve maturity at around two years of age. Others are almost three before they are fully developed.

The breeder from whom you purchased your puppy will have begun accustoming him to being groomed and trimmed. Granted, there is little to do with a young Scottie, but it is important, however, that you attend to these grooming sessions regularly during the early months of your Scottie's growth. The adult coat will

It is important not to leave your puppy unoccupied for long periods of time. A puppy needs stimulation and activity to develop into a well-socialized adult.

require more of your time and more of your dog's patience. If your Scottie has been groomed regularly, you will find your task is much easier.

Diet requirements change during this growth period. Some Scotties seem as if they can never get enough to eat, while others eat just enough to avoid starving. Think of Scottie puppies as individualistic as children and act accordingly.

The amount of food you give your Scottie should be adjusted to how much he will readily consume at each meal. If the entire meal is eaten quickly, add a small amount to the next feeding and continue to do so as the need increases. This method will ensure you of giving your puppy enough food, but you must also pay close attention to the dog's appearance and condition, as you do not want a puppy to become overweight or obese.

When choosing your Scottish Terrier, watch him carefully. The way he behaves will tell you a lot about his temperament.

At eight weeks of age, a Scottie puppy is eating four meals a day. By the time he is six months old, the puppy can do well on two meals a day, with perhaps a snack in the middle of the day. If your puppy does not eat the food offered, he is either not hungry or not well. Your dog will eat when he is hungry. If you suspect the dog is not well, a trip to the veterinarian is in order.

This adolescent period is a particularly important one, as it is the time your Scottie must learn all the household and social rules by which he will live for the rest of his life. Your patience and commitment during this time will not only produce a respected canine good citizen, but will forge a bond between the two of you that will grow and ripen into a wonderful relationship. You must remember, however, that you are dealing with a rugged individualist who is not apt to respond to browbeating. The Scottie owner must be one part marine drill sergeant and one part respectful friend and equal. A hard balance to strike? Indeed, but no one said owning a Scottie was easy, just wonderful.

CARING for Your Scottie

FEEDING AND NUTRITION

The best way to make sure your Scottie puppy is obtaining the right amount and the correct type of food for his age is to follow the diet sheet provided by the breeder from whom you obtain your puppy. Do your best not to change the puppy's diet and you will be less apt to run into digestive problems and diarrhea. Diarrhea is very serious in young puppies. Puppies with diarrhea can dehydrate very rapidly, causing severe problems and even death.

If it is necessary to change your Scottie puppy's diet for any reason, it should be done gradually, over a period of several meals and a few days. Begin by adding a tablespoon or two of the new food, gradually increasing the amount until the meal consists entirely of the new product.

By the time your Scottie is 10 to 12 months old you can reduce feedings to one or two a day with a biscuit at bedtime. There are two important things to remember: Feed the meals at the same time every day and make sure what you feed is nutritionally complete.

Hard dog biscuits made especially for medium or large dogs are ideal for your Scottie. While the Scottie can certainly not be considered a "large" dog, Scottie teeth and jaws do not know

Consult your breeder or veterinarian about the appropriate diet for your Scottish Terrier.

this! These biscuits not only become highly anticipated treats to your Scottie but also are genuinely helpful in maintaining healthy gums and teeth. They are far better for your Scottie than giving him bones to chew on. Those power jaws can splinter the bones and the splinters can cause serious internal injuries.

"Balanced" Diets

In order for a canine diet to qualify as "complete and balanced" in the United States, it must meet standards set by the Subcommittee on Canine Nutrition of the National

A healthy Scottie will look forward to mealtime! Looks like Oliver, owned by Joe Barnett, is eager to get those plates on the dinner table.

There are a number of quality dog foods and treats available that will offer special nutritional value to your growing puppy.

Research Council of the National Academy of Sciences. Most commercial foods manufactured for dogs meet these standards and prove this by listing the ingredients contained in the food on every package or can. The ingredients are listed in descending order with the main ingredient listed first.

Fed with any regularity at all, refined sugars can cause your Scottie to become obese and will definitely create tooth decay. Chocolate can be poisonous to dogs. Candy stores do not exist in the wild and canine teeth are not genetically disposed to handling sugars. Do not feed your Scottie candy or sweets and avoid products that contain sugar to any high degree. The semi-moist foods are most apt to be guilty of the latter and they are often loaded with chemical preservatives.

Make sure you have cool, clean water available to your Scottie at all times.

Never give a Scottie raw eggs. Dogs are highly susceptible to salmonella poisoning and the white of the egg can interfere with proper absorption of the vitamins contained in the good food you are giving your Scottie.

Fresh water and a properly prepared, balanced diet containing the essential nutrients in correct proportions are all a healthy Scottie should be offered. Dog foods come canned, dry, semi-moist, "scientifically fortified" and "all-natural." A visit to your local supermarket or pet store will reveal a vast array from which you will be able to select. However, feeding a dry kibble rather than semi-most or canned food is highly recommended.

It is important to remember all dogs, whether they are Scotties or Great Danes, are carnivorous (meat-eating) animals. While the vegetable content of your Scottie's diet should not be overlooked, a dog's physiology and anatomy are based upon carnivorous food acquisition. Protein and fat are absolutely

It is important to feed your Scottie a well-balanced diet in order to keep him healthy and happy.

essential to the well being of your Scottie.

Read the list of ingredients on the dog food you buy. Animal protein should appear first on the label's list of ingredients. A base of quality kibble to which only a tablespoon or so of meat has been added can provide a nutritious meal for your Scottie.

This having been said, it should be realized that in the wild, carnivores eat the entire beast they capture and kill. The carnivore's kills consist almost entirely of herbivorous (plant eating) animals and, invariably, the carnivore begins its meal with the contents of the herbivore's stomach. This provides the carbohydrates, minerals, and nutrients present in vegetables.

Through centuries of domestication, we have made our dogs entirely dependent upon us for their well being. Therefore, we are entirely responsible for duplicating the food balance the wild dog finds in nature. The domesticated dog's diet must include protein, carbohydrates, fats, roughage, and small amounts of essential minerals and vitamins.

Finding commercially prepared diets that contain all the necessary nutrients will not present a problem. It is important to understand, though, that these commercially prepared foods do contain all the necessary nutrients your Scottie needs. It is therefore unnecessary to add all the vitamin supplements to these diets the advertisements indicate are "essential." A single daily multiple vitamin may be recommended by your veterinarian in some cases. Oversupplementation and forced growth are now looked upon by some breeders as major contributors to many skeletal abnormalities found in the purebred dogs of the day.

Oversupplementation

A great deal of controversy exists today regarding the orthopedic problems that inflict many of the canine breeds. Some claim these problems are entirely hereditary conditions, but many others feel they can be exacerbated by the overuse of mineral and vitamin supplements for puppies.

In giving any vitamin supplementation, one should never exceed the prescribed amount. Many breeders insist all recommended dosages be halved before including them in a dog's diet.

Pregnant and lactating bitches usually require supplementation of some kind but, here again, it is not a case of "if a little is good, a lot would be a great deal better." Extreme caution is advised in this case and best discussed with your veterinarian.

A Scottie that becomes accustomed to being hand fed from the table can become a real pest at meal time very quickly. This invariably leads to your dog's development of finicky eating habits, to say nothing of the fact that your dinner guests may find the pleading stare of your Scottie less than appealing.

Dogs do not care if food looks like a hot dog or a piece of cheese. Truly nutritious dog foods are seldom manufactured to look like food that appeals to humans. Dogs only care about how food smells and tastes. It is highly doubtful you will be eating your dog's food, so do not waste your money on these "looks just like" products.

Along these lines, most of the moist foods or canned foods that have the look of "delicious red beef" look that way because they contain great amounts of red dyes as well as sugar. They should not be fed to a Scottie! Preservatives, dyes, and sugars are no better for your dog than they are for you.

Special Diets

There are numbers of commercially prepared diets for dogs with special dietary needs. The overweight, underweight, or geriatric dog can have his nutritional needs met as can puppies and growing dogs. The calorie content of these foods is adjusted accordingly. With the correct amount of the right foods and the proper amount of exercise, your Scottie should stay in top shape. Again, common sense must prevail. Too many calories will increase weight—fewer calories will reduce weight.

Occasionally, a young Scottie going through the teething period will become a poor eater. The concerned owner's first response is to tempt the dog by hand feeding special treats and foods that the problem eater seems to prefer. This practice only serves to compound the problem. Once the dog learns to play the waiting game, he will turn up his nose at anything

Scottish Terriers require some vegetable matter in their diet. The Carrot Bone™, made by Nylabone®, helps control plaque, eases the need to chew, and is nutritious. It is highly recommended as a healthy toy for your Scottie.

other than his favorite food, knowing full well what he wants to eat will eventually arrive.

Unlike humans, dogs have no suicidal tendencies. A healthy dog will not starve himself to death. He may not eat enough to keep himself in the shape we find ideal and attractive, but he will definitely eat enough to maintain himself. If your Scottie is not eating properly and appears to be too thin, it is probably best to consult your veterinarian.

SPECIAL NEEDS OF THE SCOTTIE

Exercise

If your own exercise proclivities lie closer to a walk around the block than to ten mile runs, your choice of a Scottie was probably a wise one. The Scottie is not a breed that requires taking your energy level to its outer limits. In fact, if your Scottie shares his life with young children or other dogs, he could easily be getting all the exercise he needs to stay fit. A Scottie is always ready for a romp or even to invent some new game that entails plenty of aerobic activity. His inquisitive nature requires the Scottie to check out every sound and movement that occurs within his territory and that alone requires a good many steps per day!

This does not mean that your Scottie will not benefit from a brisk daily walk around the park. Slow steady exercise that keeps your companion's heart rate working will do nothing but extend his life. If your Scottie is doing all this with you at his side, you are increasing the chances that the two of you will enjoy each other's company for many more years to come.

Scotties are energetic and inquisitive. They will investigate and explore everything within their realm.

Naturally, common sense must be used in the extent and the intensity of the exercise you give your Scottie. Remember, young puppies have short bursts of energy and then require long rest periods. No puppy of any breed should be forced to accompany you on extended runs—serious injuries can result. Again, short exercise periods and long rest stops for any Scottie under one year of age.

This Scottie may look cold, but because of their thick, coarse coats they quite enjoy the brisk weather.

Most adult Scotties will willingly walk as far, perhaps farther, than their owners are inclined to go. Daily walks combined with some ball retrieving or game playing in the yard can keep the average Scottie in fine fettle.

The Scottish Terrier is an active and energetic dog who will benefit greatly from a brisk daily walk around the neighborhood.

Weather

Caution must be exercised in hot weather. First of all, the Scottie is not a breed that enjoys being exposed to hot summer sun. Black absorbs heat and the

darker colored your Scottie is, the more susceptible he will be to overheating. During hot weather, plan your walks for the first thing in the morning if at all possible. If you cannot arrange to do this, wait until the sun has set and the outdoor temperature has dropped to a comfortable degree.

You must never leave your Scottie in a car in hot weather. Temperatures can soar in a matter of minutes and your dog can die of heat exhaustion in less time than you would ever imagine. Rolling down the windows helps little and is dangerous in that an over-heated Scottie will panic and attempt to escape through the open window. A word to the wise—leave your Scottie at home in a cool room on hot days.

The Scottie is by nature a happy dog that enjoys the company of others!

Cold weather, even temperatures hovering around the zero mark, is no problem at all for the active Scottie for short periods of time. The only warm clothing required for your winter walks will be yours, as long as the two of you keep moving. Do not, however, allow your Scottie to remain wet if the two of you get caught in the rain. At the very least, you should towel dry the wet Scottie. Better still, use your blow dryer to make sure your Scottie is thoroughly dry should he become wet during cold weather.

Socialization

The Scottie is by nature a happy dog and takes most situations in stride, but it is important to accommodate the breed's natural instincts by making sure your dog is accustomed to everyday events of all kinds. Traffic, strange noises, loud or hyperactive children, and strange animals can be very intimidating to a dog of any breed that has never experienced them before. Gently and gradually introduce your Scottie puppy to as many strange situations as you possibly can.

If you introduce your Scottish Terrier to other pets in your household while he is still young, he will make friends that last a lifetime.

TRAINING Your Scottish Terrier

There is no breed of dog that cannot be trained. It does appear that some breeds are more difficult to get the desired response from than others. In many cases, however, this has more to do with the trainer and his or her training methods than with the dog's inability to learn. With the proper approach, any dog that is not mentally deficient can be taught to be a good canine citizen. Many dog owners do not understand how a dog learns, nor do they realize they can be breed specific in their approach to training.

Young puppies have an amazing capacity to learn. This capacity is greater than most humans realize. It is important to remember, though, that these young puppies also forget with great speed unless they are reminded of what they have learned by continual reinforcement.

As puppies leave the nest, they began their search for two things; a pack leader and the rules set down by that leader by

Puppies are naturally mischievous and playful. Early basic training will be much more successful if you make it fun and interesting.

Although your puppy will want to learn what you have to teach him, keep in mind that his attention span is short and he will need plenty of repetition and praise.

which the puppies can abide. Because puppies, particularly Scottie puppies, are so comical and cute, their owners fail miserably in supplying these very basic needs of every dog at the beginning of the relationship. Instead, the owner immediately begins to respond to the demands of the puppy. As soon as the strong-willed and independent Scottie finds there is no "boss" in the household, he immediately sets about establishing himself as such.

If there are no rules imposed, the puppy learns to make his own rules. And, unfortunately, the negligent owner continually reinforces the puppy's decisions by allowing him to govern the household.

With small dogs like the Scottie, this scenario can produce a neurotic nuisance. In large dogs, the situation can be downright dangerous. Neither situation is an acceptable one.

Bonding is by far one of the most important building blocks of training. "Jackson" revels in the love and attention he gets from his owner, Josephine Musson.

The key to successful training lies in establishing the proper relationship between dog and owner. The owner or the owning family must be the pack leader and the individual or family must provide the rules by which the dog abides.

Once this is established, ease of training depends upon just how much a dog wants his master's approval. The entirely dependent dog lives to please his master and will do everything in his power to evoke the approval response from the person to whom he is devoted.

At the opposite end of the pole, we have the totally independent dog that is not deeply concerned with what his master thinks. Dependency varies from one breed to the next and to a degree within breeds as well. Scotties are no exception to this rule and they provide a challenge to the trainer in that they are very independent critters! This is not to say the Scottie is not a loving dog. On the contrary, the Scottie's owner is one of the most important things in his life. However, that love will never translate into slavish behavior.

HOUSEBREAKING

A major key to successfully training your Scottie, whether it is obedience training or housebreaking, is avoidance. It is much easier for your Scottie to learn something if you do not first have to convince the puppy he must unlearn some bad habit. (Remember your Scottie's determined attitude!) The "crate" or "denning" method of housebreaking is a highly successful method of preventing bad habits.

A healthy and tasty treat for your Scottish Terrier because they love cheese is CHOOZ™. CHOOZ™ are bone-hard but can be microwaved to expand into a huge, crispy dog biscuit. They are almost fat free and about 70% protein.

First-time dog owners are inclined to initially see the crate/denning method as cruel but those same people will return later and thank a breeder profusely for having suggested it in the first place. New owners are also surprised to find that the puppy will eventually come to think of his crate as a place of private retreat—his den if you will, to which he will retire for rest and privacy. The success of this method is based upon the fact that puppies will not soil the area in which they sleep unless they are forced.

Use of a crate reduces housetraining time down to an absolute minimum and avoids keeping a puppy under constant stress by incessantly correcting him for making mistakes in the house. The anti-crate advocates consider it cruel to confine a puppy for any length of time, but find no problem in constantly harassing and punishing the puppy because he has wet on the carpet or relieved himself behind the sofa.

Crates come in a wide variety of styles. The fiberglass shipping kennels used by many airlines are popular with most Scottie owners, but residents of the warmer climates sometimes prefer the wire-cage type. Both are available at pet stores.

There are many sizes to choose from as well. The medium size of fiberglass crate (approximately 19 inches high by 20 inches wide by 27 inches long) seems ideal for most Scotties.

The crate used for housebreaking should be large enough for the puppy to stand up and lie down in and stretch out comfortably. It is not necessary to dash out and buy a new crate every few weeks to accommodate the Scottie's rapid spurts of growth. Simply cut a piece of plywood to partition off the excess space in the very large crate and move it back as needed. Long before you have lost the need for the partition, your Scottie will be housebroken.

Begin by feeding your puppy in his crate. Keep the door closed and latched while the puppy is eating. When the meal is finished, open the crate and carry the puppy outdoors to the spot where you want him to learn to eliminate. In the event you do not have outdoor access or will be away from home for long periods of time, begin housebreaking by placing newspapers in some out of the way corner that is easily accessible to the puppy. If you consistently take your puppy to the same spot, you will reinforce the habit of going there for that purpose.

This Scottie puppy is so comfortable inside his crate that he can set his mind to other things—like making mischief!

It is important that you do not let the puppy loose after eating. Young puppies will eliminate almost immediately after eating or drinking. They will also be ready to relieve themselves when they first wake up and after playing. If you keep a watchful eye on your puppy, you will quickly learn when this is about to take place. A puppy usually circles and sniffs the floor just before he will relieve himself. Do not give your puppy an opportunity to learn that he can eliminate in the house! Your housetraining chores will be reduced considerably if you avoid this happening in the first place.

Crates make housetraining your pet much easier, because dogs do not want to soil where they eat and sleep.

If you are not able to watch your puppy every minute, he should be in his crate with the door securely latched. Each time you put your puppy in the crate, give him a small treat of some kind. Throw the treat to the back of the crate and encourage the puppy to walk in on his own. When he does so praise the puppy and perhaps hand him another piece of the treat through the opening in the front of the crate.

Do not succumb to your puppy's complaints about being in his crate. The puppy must learn to stay there and to do so without unnecessary complaining. A quick "no" command and a tap on the crate will usually get the puppy to understand theatrics will not result in liberation. (Remember, you, the pack leader, make the rules and the puppy is seeking to learn what they are!)

Do understand that a puppy of 10 to 12 weeks of age will not be able to contain himself for long periods of time. Puppies of that age must relieve themselves every few hours except at night. Your schedule must be adjusted accordingly. Also, make sure your puppy has relieved himself, both bowel and bladder, the last thing at night and do not dawdle when you wake up in the morning.

Your first priority in the morning is to get the puppy outdoors. Just how early this ritual will take place will depend much more upon your puppy than upon you. If your Scottie is like most others, there will be no doubt in your mind when he needs to be let out. You will also very quickly learn to tell the difference between the "this is an emergency" complaint and the "I just want out" grumbling. Do not test the young puppy's ability to contain himself. His vocal demands to be let out are confirmation that the housebreaking lesson is being learned.

Should you find it necessary to be away from home all day, you will not be able to leave your puppy in a crate, but on the other hand, do not make the mistake of allowing him to roam the house or even a large room at will. Confine the puppy to a very small room or partitioned-off area and cover the floor with newspaper. Make this area large enough so that the puppy will not have to relieve himself next to his bed, or food or water bowls. You will soon find the puppy will be inclined to use one particular spot to perform his bowel and bladder functions. When you are home, you must take the puppy to this exact spot to eliminate at the appropriate time.

BASIC TRAINING

Where you are emotionally and the environment in which you train is just as important to your dog's training as is his state of mind at the time. Never begin training when you are irritated, distressed, or preoccupied. Nor should you begin basic training in a place that interferes with you or your dog's concentration. Once the commands are understood and learned you can begin testing your dog in public places, but at first the two of you should work in a place where you can concentrate fully upon each other.

Never resort to shaking or striking your Scottie puppy! The breed, even at a very young age, has a great sense of pride and degrading treatment will not sit well with a Scottie. A very stern "no!" at the time of the misdeed is usually more than sufficient and striking the ground with a rolled up newspaper is about as extreme as you will ever need to be.

THE NO COMMAND

There is no doubt whatsoever that one of the most important commands your Scottie puppy will ever learn is the meaning of the no command. It is critical that the puppy learns this command just as soon as possible. One important piece of advice in using this and all other commands—never give a Scottie a command you are not prepared and able to enforce! A good leader does not enforce rules arbitrarily. Since the Scottie is not inclined to obey blindly in the first place, finding you do not always mean what you say will be all he needs to convince himself that obeying is not particularly necessary. The only way a puppy learns to obey commands is to realize that once issued, commands must be obeyed. Learning the no command should start on the first day of the puppy's arrival at your home.

LEASH TRAINING

Begin leash training by putting a soft light collar on your puppy. After a few hours of occasional scratching at the unaccustomed addition, your puppy will forget it is even there.

It may not be necessary for the puppy or adult Scottie to wear his collar and identification tags within the confines of your home later, but no Scottie should ever

A young puppy will not know the difference between good and bad behavior. It is up to you, the owner, to teach him what is acceptable in your household.

leave home without a collar and without the attached leash held securely in your hand.

Begin getting your puppy accustomed to his collar by leaving it on for a few minutes at a time. Gradually extend the time you leave the collar on. Once this is accomplished, attach a lightweight leash to the collar while you are playing with the puppy. Do not try to guide the puppy at first. You are only trying to get the puppy used to having something attached to the collar.

Get your puppy to follow you as you move around by coaxing him along with a treat of some kind. Let the puppy smell what you have in your hand and then move a few steps back holding the treat in front of the puppy's nose. Just as soon as the puppy takes a few steps toward you, praise him *Every Scottish Terrier can benefit from obedience training in order to become a well-mannered pet.* enthusiastically and continue to do so as you continue to move along. Never drag your puppy along. A Scottie puppy has a brake system that will amaze you and, once the brakes are set, you may have a devil of a time getting the puppy to release them!

Make the first few lessons brief and fun for the puppy. Continue the lessons in your home or yard until the puppy is completely unconcerned about the fact that he is on a leash. With a treat in one hand and the leash in the other, you can begin to use both to guide the puppy in the direction you wish to go. Eventually the two of you can venture out on the sidewalk in front of your house and then on to adventures everywhere! This is one lesson no puppy is too young to learn.

THE COME COMMAND

The next most important lesson for the Scottie puppy to learn is to come when called. It is also the lesson when the little Scotsman may really reveal his Highland heritage and perhaps test your patience and perseverance to its limit. It is important, therefore, that the puppy first learn his name. Constant repetition is what does the trick in teaching a puppy his name. Use the name every time you talk to your puppy.

Your dog's response to his name and the word "come" should always be associated with a pleasant experience such as

great praise and petting or even a food treat. Again, remember it is much easier to avoid the establishment of bad habits than it is to correct them once set. Never give the come command unless you are sure your puppy will come to you. The very young Scottie puppy is far more inclined to respond to learning the come command than the older dog who has never had to contend with the concept. An older dog will lose that dependency and become preoccupied with his surroundings, so start your training early.

Use the command initially when the puppy is already on his way to you or give the command while walking or running away from the youngster. Clap your hands and sound very happy and excited about having the puppy join in on this "game."

POPpup's™ are healthy treats for your Scottish Terrier. When bone-hard they help to control plaque build-up; when microwaved they become a rich cracker which your Scottie will love. The POPpup™ is available in liver and other flavors and is fortified with calcium.

The very young Scottie puppy will normally want to stay as close to his owner as possible, especially in strange surroundings. When your Scottie puppy sees you moving away, his natural inclination will be to get close to you. This is a perfect time to use the come command.

You may want to attach a long leash or rope to the puppy's collar to ensure the correct response. Do not chase or punish your puppy for not obeying the come command. Doing so in the initial stages of training makes the youngster associate the command with something to fear and will undoubtedly set those famous "Scottie brakes." This will result in avoidance rather than any positive response you desire. It is imperative that you praise your Scottie puppy and give him a treat when

The time you invest in training your Scottie will benefit the both of you for a lifetime. "Katie" and "Bonnie Bell" make up a beautiful basket of Scottish cheer.

he does come to you, even if he voluntarily delays responding for many minutes.

THE SIT AND STAY COMMANDS

Just as important to your Scottie's safety as the "no" command are the "sit" and "stay" commands. Even very young Scotties can learn the sit command quickly, especially if it appears to be a game and a food treat is involved.

First, remember the Scottie-in-training should always be on collar and leash for all his lessons. A Scottie puppy is curious about everything that goes on around him and your puppy is not beyond getting up and walking away when he has decided he needs to investigate something.

Give the sit command just before you reach down and exert pressure on your puppy's rear. Praise the puppy profusely when he does sit, even though it was you who made him exert the effort. A food treat of some kind always seems to make the experience more enjoyable for the puppy.

Continue holding the dog's rear end down and repeat the sit command several times. If your puppy makes an attempt to get up, repeat the command yet again while exerting pressure on the rear end until the correct position is assumed. Make your puppy stay in this position a little bit longer with each succeeding lesson. Begin with a few seconds and increase the time as lessons progress over the following weeks.

Should your puppy attempt to get up or lie down, he should be corrected by simply saying, "sit!" in a firm voice. This should be accompanied by returning the dog to the desired position. Only when you decide your dog should get up should he be allowed to do so. Do not test the young Scottie puppy's patience to the limits. Remember you are dealing with a baby, first and a Scottie, second. The attention span of any youngster is relatively limited. The Scottie puppy is certainly no exception.

When you do decide the dog can get up, call his name, say "okay" and make a big fuss over him. Praise and a food treat are in order every time your Scottie responds correctly.

Once your puppy has mastered the sit lesson you may start on the stay command. With your Scottie on leash and facing you, command him to sit, then take a step or two backward. If your dog attempts to get up to follow, firmly say, "Sit, stay!" While you are saying this, raise your hand, palm toward the dog, and again command "Stay!"

If your dog attempts to get up, you must correct him at once, returning him to the sit position and repeat, "Stay!" Once your Scottie begins to understand what you want, you can gradually increase the distance you step back. With a long leash attached to your dog's collar, start with a few steps and gradually increase the

Look at those sad puppy eyes! Be sure to offer your Scottie plenty of positive reinforcement and in no time at all he'll be obeying every command.

If you are patient and consistent when training your puppy, you'll have a well-behaved adult Scottie as a reward.

distance to several yards. With advanced training, your Scottie can be taught the command is to be obeyed even when you leave the room or are entirely out of sight.

As your Scottie becomes accustomed to responding to this lesson and is able to remain in the sit position for as long as you command, do not end the command by calling the dog to you. Walk back to your Scottie and say "okay." This will let your dog know the command is over. When your Scottie becomes entirely dependable, you can then call the dog to you.

The sit/stay command can take considerable time and patience to get across to puppies. You must not forget their attention span will be short. Keep the stay part of the lesson very short until your puppy is about six months old.

THE DOWN COMMAND

Do not try and teach your Scottie puppy too many things at once. Wait until you have mastered one lesson quite well before moving on to something new.

When you feel quite confident that your Scottie puppy is comfortable with the sit and stay commands, you can start work on down. This is the single word command for "lie down." Use the down command only when you want the dog to lie down. If you want your Scottie to get off your sofa or to stop jumping up on people, use the off command. Do not interchange these two commands. Doing so will only serve to confuse your dog and evoking the right response will become next to impossible.

The down position is especially useful if you want your Scottie to remain in one place for a long period of time. Most dogs are far more inclined to stay put when lying down than when they are sitting or standing.

Teaching this command to your Scottie may take more time and patience than the previous lessons the two of you have undertaken. It is believed by some animal behaviorists that assuming the down position somehow represents greater submissiveness.

With your Scottie sitting in front of and facing you, hold a treat in your right hand with the excess part of the leash in your left hand. Hold the treat under the dog's nose and slowly bring your hand down to the ground. Your dog will follow the treat with his head and neck. As he does, give the command "down" and exert light pressure on the dog's shoulders with your left hand. If your dog resists the pressure on his shoulders, do not continue pushing down, as doing so will only create more resistance. Reach down and slide the dog's feet toward you until he is lying down.

An alternative method of getting your Scottie headed into the down position is to move around to the dog's right side, and as you do, draw his attention downward with your right hand. Slide your left hand under the dog's front legs and gently slide the legs forward. You will undoubtedly have to be on your knees next to the youngster in order to do so.

As your Scottie's forelegs begin to slide out to his front, keep moving the treat along the ground until the dog's whole body is lying on the ground while you continually repeat "down." Once your dog has assumed the position you desire, give him the treat and a lot of praise. Continue assisting your Scottie into the down position until he does so on his own. Be firm and be patient.

The HERCULES™ is made of very tough polyurethane. It is designed for Scottish Terriers who are extremely strong chewers. The raised dental tips massage the gums and mechanically remove the plaque they encounter during chewing.

THE HEEL COMMAND

In learning to heel, your Scottie will walk on your left side with his shoulder next to your leg, no matter which direction you might go or how quickly you turn. Teaching your Scottie to heel will not only make your daily walks far more enjoyable, it will make a far more tractable companion when the two of you are in crowded or confusing situations. We do not recommend ever allowing your Scottie to be off leash when you are away from home, but it is important to know you can control your dog no matter what the circumstances.

A lightweight, link-chain, training collar is best to use for the heeling lesson and changing to this collar for the lesson indicates what you are doing is "business" and not just a casual stroll. These link-chain collars provide quick pressure around the neck and a snapping sound, both of which get a dog's attention. These collars are called "choke collars" by some people, but rest assured when the link-chain collar is used properly, it will not choke the dog. The pet shop at which you purchase the training collar will be able to show you the proper way to put this collar on your dog.

As you train your Scottie puppy to walk along on the leash, you should accustom the youngster to walk on your left side. The leash should cross your body from the dog's collar to your right hand. The excess portion of the leash will be folded into your right hand and your left hand will be used to make corrections with the leash.

A quick short jerk on the leash with your left hand will keep your Scottie from lunging from side to side, pulling ahead, or lagging back. As you make a correction, give the "heel" command. Keep the leash loose when the dog maintains the proper position at your side.

If your dog begins to drift away, give the leash a quick jerk and guide the dog back to the correct position and give the heel command. Do not pull on the lead with steady pressure. What is needed is a sharp but gentle jerking motion to get your dog's attention.

TRAINING CLASSES

There are few limits to what a patient consistent Scottie owner can teach his or her dog. Many Scottie owners feel the more the Scottie learns, the more he wants to learn. However, remember the breed's heritage. The Scotsman is not about to be bullied.

For advanced obedience work beyond the basics, it is wise for the Scottie owner to consider local professional assistance. Professional trainers have had long-standing experience in avoiding the pitfalls of obedience training and can help you to avoid them as well.

Don't let life pass your Scotties by! Proper training will allow them to participate in all the excitement life has to offer!

This training assistance can be obtained in many ways. Classes are particularly good in that your dog is learning to obey commands in spite of all the interesting sights and smells of other dogs. There are free-of-charge classes at many parks and recreation facilities, as well as very formal and sometimes very expensive individual lessons with private trainers.

A terrier by nature, the Scottie will investigate anything in his path.

There are also some obedience schools that will take your Scottie and train him for you. However, having someone else train the dog for you would be last on our list of recommendations. The Scottie responds best to his owner, and a stranger trying to tell your dog what to do will have far less, if any, lasting results. The rapport that develops between the owner who has trained his or her Scottie and the dog is incomparable. The effort you expend to teach your dog to be a pleasant companion and good canine citizen pays off in years of enjoyable companionship.

Group training sessions will allow your puppy to make friends and are a wonderful way to continue your puppy's socialization.

GROOMING Your Scottish Terrier

Much of what initially attracts people to the Scottie is his jaunty tailored look. We wish we could tell you that look is a natural part of the breed's inheritance. Unfortunately, it is not. Your Scottie will only maintain that special look as long as you are diligent in keeping his coat thoroughly brushed, his beard and whiskers clean, and either learn to trim him yourself or find a talented groomer. This cannot be accomplished by occasional attacks on the problem after long periods of neglect.

The damage done by neglecting the Scottie's coat can normally

Your new Scottie puppy will look to you, his owner, to provide for all his grooming needs.

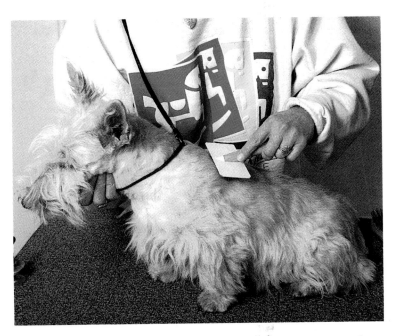

If you accustom your Scottie to grooming procedures at an early age, he will come to think of it as a pleasant experience.

only be undone by shaving away the dog's coat because of the mats that have developed.

This is neither attractive nor is it good for your dog. If you are not willing to put in the time and effort necessary to maintain the Scottie's coat, which to a great extent constitutes a part of his very essence, why not get a smooth-coated dog instead?

Do not think you are doing your dog a favor by shaving him. The Scottie's coat insulates against both heat and cold. Shaving your dog to keep him cool for the summer months is working against the breed's natural defense against soaring temperatures.

Puppy Coat

Undoubtedly the breeder from whom you purchased your Scottie will have begun to accustom the puppy to grooming just as soon as there was enough hair to brush. You must continue on with grooming sessions or begin them at once if for some reason they have not been started. It is imperative

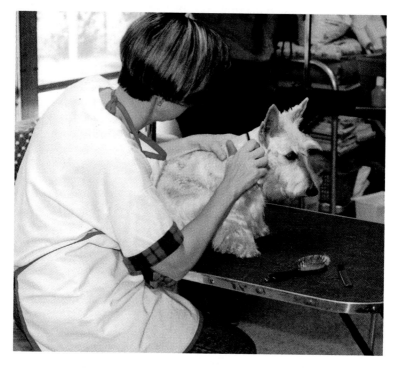

Ch. Boldmere's Cakewalk looks perfectly at home on the grooming table, getting a touch-up from her owner Lois Bolding.

you both learn to cooperate in the endeavor to make it an easy and pleasant experience.

The first piece of equipment you will have to obtain is a grooming table that has an arm and noose attached to it. The noose slips around your dog's neck and once your Scottie becomes accustomed to the device, it will eliminate much of the fidgeting and attempting to escape the dog might do otherwise. It is amazing how patient the well-trained Scottie can be when he wants to be, but do not go away and leave your Scottie unattended with the noose around his neck. The dog may attempt to jump down and could seriously damage his neck or even strangle himself.

Make sure that whatever kind of table you use, it is of a height at which you can work comfortably. Adjustable-height grooming tables are available at most pet shops. Although you will buy this when your Scottie puppy first arrives, anticipate his full-grown size in making your purchase and select or build a table that will accommodate a fully grown Scottie lying down.

Proper grooming for the show ring takes a great deal of time and many years of practice. The Scottish Terrier Club of America has published a step-by-step grooming guide for those who wish to learn how to do a Scottie show trim. If you have purchased a show-quality puppy, the breeder of the puppy will assist you in this respect as well, but our advice would be to seek professional help for show grooming until you have become proficient yourself.

Ch. Hycourt High Tea at Boldmere has been brushed and trimmed and is now ready for her first turn in the show ring at nine months of age.

Pet grooming is much easier, but still requires the necessary grooming tools. The tools needed for the pet trim are: electric animal clippers, barber scissors, thinning shears, nail clippers, a pin brush, and a steel comb. A soft bristle brush is very helpful for the finishing touches on the topcoat. A hair dryer designed for human use is perfectly fine to use on your dog after he is bathed and your local pet shop will be able to assist you in obtaining the proper tools.

Consider the fact that you will be using this equipment for many years, so buy the best of these items that you can afford.

It is important to accustom your puppy to the sounds of the electric clippers and the hair dryer. Start early with these two devices, preferably before you really have to use them for the first time. Begin by turning one or the other on and allowing the puppy to become used to the sounds. Eventually move the clippers closer to the puppy so that he becomes accustomed to the vibration. In the case of the hair dryer, once the puppy is accustomed to the sound, begin to gently and gradually turn the air flow toward the puppy. All this should be accompanied by great praise and perhaps even a treat, rewarding the puppy for his bravery in the face of such great "danger."

Do not wait until you want to actually begin to use these tools before you introduce them to the puppy. It is difficult enough to hold a squirming puppy still that is accustomed to the sounds and vibrations of the tools. It will be impossible to do your work if the puppy has never seen or heard the sounds before!

Do not attempt to groom your puppy on the floor. The puppy will only attempt to get away from you when he has decided enough is enough and you will spend a good part of your time chasing the puppy around the room. Also, sitting on the floor for long stretches of time is not the most comfortable position in the world for the average adult.

Before you begin trimming of any kind, you must brush your Scottie's coat thoroughly to be sure it is mat free.

Before you begin trimming of any kind, you must make sure your Scottie's coat is mat free. Should you encounter a mat that does not brush out easily, use your fingers and the steel comb to separate the hairs as much as possible. Do not cut or pull out the matted hair. Apply baby powder or one of the especially prepared grooming powders directly to the mat and brush completely from the skin out.

When combing or brushing on and around the rear legs, make sure to give special attention to the area of the anus and genitalia. Needless to say, it is important to be extremely careful when brushing in these areas for they are very sensitive and easily injured.

Establish a grooming routine early in your dog's life. Procedures like nail clipping will be far easier with a willing participant.

NAIL TRIMMING

This is a good time to accustom your Scottie to having his nails trimmed and his feet inspected. Not only will your puppy intensely dislike this part of his toilette, it is difficult for the groomer as well. The Scottie's nails are black and it is extremely difficult to see the blood vessel running through the center of the nail and into the "quick." The quick grows close to the end of the nail and contains very sensitive nerve endings. If the nail is allowed to grow too long, it will be impossible to cut it back to a proper length without cutting into the quick. This can cause severe pain to the dog and can also result in a great deal of bleeding that can be very difficult to stop.

It may take hard work to achieve the Scottie's jaunty and tailored look, but remember a well-groomed dog is a healthy dog, and a healthy dog is a happy dog!

The nails of a Scottie who spends most of his time indoors or on grass when outdoors can grow long very quickly. Do not allow the nails to become overgrown and then expect to cut them back easily. If your Scottie is getting plenty of exercise on cement or rough hard pavement, the nails may keep sufficiently worn down. Otherwise the nails can grow long very quickly. They must then be carefully trimmed back.

Should the quick be nipped in the trimming process, there are any number of blood clotting products available at pet shops that will almost immediately stem the flow of blood. It is wise to have one of these products on hand in case there is a nail trimming accident or the dog tears a nail on his own.

There are coarse metal files available at your pet emporium or hardware store that can be used in place of the nail clippers. This is a more gradual method of taking the nail back and one is far less apt to injure the quick.

Always inspect your dog's feet for cracked pads. Check between the toes for splinters

When bathing your Scottie place a dab of mineral oil or petroleum jelly in each eye to prevent any shampoo irritation.

and thorns. Pay particular attention to any swollen or tender areas. In many sections of the country, there is a weed that releases a small barbed hook that carries its seed. This hook can easily find its way into a Scottie's foot or between his toes and very quickly works its way deep into the dog's flesh. This will very quickly cause soreness and infection. These barbs should be removed by your veterinarian before serious problems result.

CLIPPING

With a picture of a well-groomed Scottie in front of you, your job will be to attempt to duplicate the breed "look" with scissors and electric clippers. The hair of the head and back coat are trimmed with the clippers. The remainder of the hair is trimmed and shaped with thinning shears.

It is seriously suggested that the owner who plans on doing his or her own grooming sit through a grooming session or two at a professional grooming shop that has had experience in doing pet trims for Scotties. What may seem like an unfathomable mystery becomes relatively more simple if one has watched it accomplished a time or two.

BATHING

If your Scottie is given regular and thorough brushing sessions every few days, it will not be necessary to bathe him with any great frequency. Actually, the less the better. There are many dry cleaning products on the market today that if used according to the directions, will keep your Scottie's coat

clean and fresh smelling, eliminating all doggie odor. If you do bathe your Scottie, he should never be bathed until after he has been thoroughly brushed. The mats will only get worse when wet.

A small cotton ball placed inside each ear will avoid water

Be sure to trim all the hair between your Scottie's pads well during grooming.

Charthill's Woodland Path takes an admiring look at her well-groomed coat in the mirror and seems to approve!

running down into the dog's ear canal and a drop or two of mineral oil or a dab of petroleum jelly placed in each eye will stop shampoo from irritating the Scottie's eyes.

It is best to use a shampoo designed especially for dogs. In bathing, start behind the ears and work back. Use a wash cloth to soap and rinse around the head and face. Once you have shampooed your Scottie, you must rinse the coat thoroughly and, when you feel quite certain all shampoo residue has been removed, rinse once more. Shampoo residue in the coat is sure to dry the hair and cause skin irritation.

As soon as you have completed the bath, use heavy towels to remove as much of the excess water as possible. Your Scottie will assist you in the process by shaking a great deal of the water out of his coat on his own.

It is best to "brush dry" your Scottie using your pin brush and a hair dryer. Right after a quick towel drying, use your pin brush to go through the damp coat to remove any tangles and then continue on brushing with the lay of the hair. Always set your hair dryer at "medium" setting, never "hot." The hot setting may be quicker but it will also dry out the hair and could easily burn the skin of your Scottie.

SPORT of Purebred Dogs

Welcome to the exciting and sometimes frustrating sport of dogs. No doubt you are trying to learn more about dogs or you wouldn't be deep into this book. This section covers the basics that may entice you, further your knowledge and help you to understand the dog world.

Dog showing has been a very popular sport for a long time and has been taken quite seriously by some. Others only enjoy it as a hobby.

The Kennel Club in England was formed in 1859, the American Kennel Club was established in 1884 and the Canadian Kennel Club was formed in 1888. The purpose of these clubs was to register purebred dogs and maintain their Stud Books. In the beginning, the concept of registering dogs was not readily accepted. More than 36 million dogs have been enrolled in the AKC Stud Book since its inception in 1888. Presently the kennel clubs not only register dogs but adopt and enforce rules and regulations governing dog shows, obedience trials and field trials. Over the years they have fostered and encouraged interest in the health and welfare of the purebred dog. They routinely donate funds to veterinary research for study on genetic disorders.

Below are the addresses of the kennel clubs in the United States, Great Britain and Canada.

The American Kennel Club
51 Madison Avenue
New York, NY 10010
(Their registry is located at: 5580 Centerview Drive, STE 200, Raleigh, NC 27606-3390)

The Kennel Club
1 Clarges Street
Piccadilly, London, WIY 8AB, England

The Canadian Kennel Club
111 Eglinton Avenue
East Toronto, Ontario M6S 4V7
Canada

Today there are numerous activities that are enjoyable for both the dog and the handler. Some of the activities include conformation showing, obedience competition, tracking, agility, the Canine Good Citizen Certificate, and a wide range of instinct tests that vary from breed to breed. Where you start depends upon your goals which early on may not be readily apparent.

Puppy Kindergarten

Every puppy will benefit from this class. PKT is the foundation for all future dog activities from conformation to "couch potatoes." Pet owners should make an effort to attend even if they never expect to show their dog. The class is designed for puppies about three months

Although he is too young now, someday Josephine Musson's little Markus will be well trained and know that toes are not snack food!

of age with graduation at approximately five months of age. All the puppies will be in the same age group and, even though some may be a little unruly, there should not be any real problem. This class will teach the puppy some beginning obedience. As in all obedience classes the owner learns how to train his own dog. The PKT class gives the puppy the opportunity to interact with other puppies in the same age group and exposes him to strangers, which is very important. Some dogs grow up with behavior problems, one of them being fear of strangers. As you can see, there can be much to gain from this class.

There are some basic obedience exercises that every dog should learn. Some of these can be started with puppy kindergarten.

Sit

One way of teaching the sit is to have your dog on your left side with the leash in your right hand, close to the collar. Pull up on the leash and at the same time reach around his hindlegs with your left hand and tuck them in. As you are doing this say, "Beau, sit." Always use the dog's name when you give an active command. Some owners like to use a treat holding it over the dog's head. The dog will need to sit to get the treat. Encourage the dog to hold the sit for a few seconds, which will eventually be the beginning of the Sit/Stay. Depending on how cooperative he is, you can rub him under the chin or stroke his back. It is a good time to establish eye contact.

Down

Sit the dog on your left side and kneel down beside him with the leash in your right hand. Reach over him with your

A well-socialized Scottie will enjoy the company of other dogs.

left hand and grasp his left foreleg. With your right hand, take his right foreleg and pull his legs forward while you say, "Beau, down." If he tries to get up, lean on his shoulder to encourage him to stay down. It will relax your dog if you stroke his back while he is down. Try to encourage him to stay down for a few seconds as preparation for the Down/Stay.

All Scottish Terriers benefit from early training to teach them basic obedience and good manners.

Heel

The definition of heeling is the dog walking under control at your left heel. Your puppy will learn controlled walking in the puppy kindergarten class, which will eventually lead to heeling. The command is "Beau, heel," and you start off briskly with your left foot. Your leash is in your right hand and your left hand is holding it about half way down. Your left hand should be able to control the leash and there should be a little slack in it. You want him to walk with you with your leg somewhere between his nose and his shoulder. You need to encourage him to stay with you, not forging (in front of you) or lagging behind you. It is best to keep him on a fairly short lead. Do not allow the lead to become tight. It is far better to give him a little jerk when necessary and remind him to heel. When you come to a halt, be prepared physically to make him sit. It takes practice to become coordinated. There are excellent books on training that you may wish to purchase. Your instructor should be able to recommend one for you.

Recall

This quite possibly is the most important exercise you will ever teach. It should be a pleasant experience. The puppy may learn to do random recalls while being attached to a long line such as a clothes line. Later the exercise will start with the dog sitting and staying until called. The command is "Beau, come." Let your command be happy. You want your dog to come willingly and faithfully. The recall could save his life if he sneaks out the door. In practicing the recall, let him jump on you or touch you before you reach for him. If he is shy, then kneel down to his level. Reaching for the insecure dog could frighten him, and he may not be willing to come again in the future. Lots of praise and a treat would be in order whenever you do a recall. Under no circumstances should you ever correct your dog when he has come to you. Later in formal obedience your dog will be required to sit in front of you after recalling and then go to heel position.

CONFORMATION

Conformation showing is our oldest dog show sport. This type of showing is based on the dog's appearance—that is his structure, movement and attitude. When considering this type of showing, you need to be aware of your breed's standard and be able to evaluate your dog compared to that standard. The breeder of your puppy or other experienced breeders would be good sources for such an

In conformation, your Scottish Terrier is judged by how closely he conforms to the breed standard.

evaluation. Puppies can go through lots of changes over a period of time. Many puppies start out as promising hopefuls and then after maturing may be disappointing as show candidates. Even so this should not deter them from being excellent pets.

Usually conformation training classes are offered by the local kennel or obedience clubs. These are excellent places for training puppies. The puppy should be able to walk on a lead before entering such a class. Proper ring procedure and technique for posing (stacking) the dog will be demonstrated as well as gaiting the dog. Usually certain patterns are used in the ring such as the triangle or the "L." Conformation class, like the PKT class, will give your youngster the opportunity to socialize with different breeds of dogs and humans too.

What a natural! Four-month-old Annette, owned by Lois Bolding, strikes a perfect pose.

It takes some time to learn the routine of conformation showing. Usually one starts at the puppy matches that may be AKC Sanctioned or Fun Matches. These matches are generally for puppies from two or three months to a year old, and there may be classes for the adult over the age of 12 months. Similar to point shows, the classes are divided by sex and after completion of the classes in that breed or variety, the class winners compete for Best of Breed or Variety. The winner goes on to compete in the Group and the Group winners compete for Best in Match. No championship points are awarded for match wins.

A few matches can be great training for puppies even though there is no intention to go on showing. Matches enable the puppy to meet new people and be handled by a stranger—the judge. It is also a change of environment, which broadens the horizon for both dog and handler. Matches and other dog activities boost the confidence of the handler and especially the younger handlers.

Earning an AKC championship is built on a point system, which is different from Great Britain. To become an AKC Champion of Record the dog must earn 15 points. The number

Handlers must pose their Scottish Terriers in the most flattering position to emphasize the dog's specific strengths.

of points earned each time depends upon the number of dogs in competition. The number of points available at each show depends upon the breed, its sex and the location of the show. The United States is divided into ten AKC zones. Each zone has its own set of points. The purpose of the zones is to try to equalize the points available from breed to breed and area to area. The AKC adjusts the point scale annually.

The number of points that can be won at a show are between one and five. Three-, four- and five-point wins are considered majors. Not only does the dog need 15 points won under three different judges, but those points must include two majors under two different judges. Canada also works on a point system but majors are not required.

Dogs always show before bitches. The classes available to those seeking points are: Puppy (which may be divided into 6 to 9 months and 9 to 12 months); 12 to 18 months; Novice; Bred-by-Exhibitor; American-bred; and Open. The class winners of the same sex of each breed or variety compete against each other for Winners Dog and Winners Bitch. A

Reserve Winners Dog and Reserve Winners Bitch are also awarded but do not carry any points unless the Winners win is disallowed by AKC. The Winners Dog and Bitch compete with the specials (those dogs that have attained championship) for Best of Breed or Variety, Best of Winners and Best of Opposite Sex. It is possible to pick up an extra point or even a major if the points are higher for the defeated winner than those of Best of Winners. The latter would get the higher total from the defeated winner.

Successful showing requires dedication and preparation, but most of all, it should be an enjoyable experience for handlers and dogs alike.

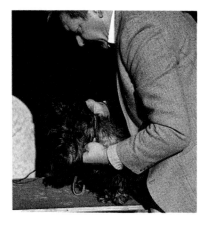

At an all-breed show, each Best of Breed or Variety winner will go on to his respective Group and then the Group winners will compete against each other for Best in Show. There are seven Groups: Sporting, Hounds, Working, Terriers, Toys, Non-Sporting and Herding. Obviously there are no Groups at speciality shows (those shows that have only one breed or a show such as the American Spaniel Club's Flushing Spaniel Show, which is for all flushing spaniel breeds).

Earning a championship in England is somewhat different since they do not have a point system. Challenge Certificates are awarded if the judge feels the dog is deserving regardless of the number of dogs in competition. A dog must earn three Challenge Certificates under three different judges, with at least one of these Certificates being won after the age of 12 months. Competition is very strong and entries may be higher than they are in the U.S. The Kennel Club's Challenge Certificates are only available at Championship Shows.

In England, The Kennel Club regulations require that certain dogs, Border Collies and Gundog breeds, qualify in a working capacity (i.e., obedience or field trials) before becoming a full Champion. If they do not qualify in the working aspect, then they are designated a Show Champion, which is equivalent to the AKC's Champion of Record. A Gundog may be granted the title of Field Trial Champion (FT Ch.) if it passes all the tests in the field but would also have to qualify in conformation before becoming a full Champion. A Border Collie that earns the title of Obedience Champion (Ob Ch.) must also qualify in the conformation ring before becoming a Champion.

The U.S. doesn't have a designation full Champion but does award for Dual and Triple Champions. The Dual Champion must be a Champion of Record, and either Champion Tracker, Herding Champion, Obedience Trial Champion or Field Champion. Any dog that has been awarded the titles of Champion of Record, and any two of the following: Champion Tracker, Herding Champion, Obedience Trial Champion or Field Champion, may be designated as a Triple Champion.

The shows in England seem to put more emphasis on breeder judges than those in the U.S. There is much competition within the breeds. Therefore the quality of the individual breeds should be very good. In the United States we tend to have more "all around judges" (those that judge multiple breeds) and use the breeder judges at the specialty shows. Breeder judges are more familiar with their own breed since they are actively breeding that breed or did so at one time. Americans emphasize Group and Best in Show wins and promote them accordingly.

The shows in England can be very large and extend over several days, with the Groups being scheduled on different days. Though multi-day shows are not common in the U.S., there are cluster shows, where several different clubs will use the same show site over consecutive days.

Westminster Kennel Club is our most prestigious show although the entry is limited to 2500. In recent years, entry has been limited to Champions. This show is more formal than the majority of the shows with the judges wearing

Good grooming is essential to a Scottie's success in the show ring.

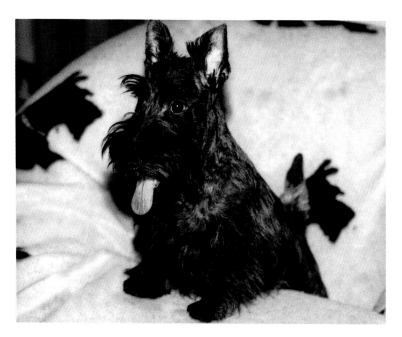

There is no telling what life has in store for your Scottie puppy. Charthill's One Tough Sailor looks like he's up for the adventure.

formal attire and the handlers fashionably dressed. In most instances the quality of the dogs is superb. After all, it is a show of Champions. It is a good show to study the AKC registered breeds and is by far the most exciting—especially since it is televised! WKC is one of the few shows in this country that is still benched. This means the dog must be in his benched area during the show hours except when he is being groomed, in the ring, or being exercised.

Typically, the handlers are very particular about their appearances. They are careful not to wear something that will detract from their dog but will perhaps enhance it. American ring procedure is quite formal compared to that of other countries. There is a certain etiquette expected between the judge and exhibitor and among the other exhibitors. Of course it is not always the case but the judge is supposed to be polite, not engaging in small talk or acknowledging how well he knows the handler. There is a more informal and relaxed atmosphere at the shows in other countries. For instance, the dress code is more casual. I can see where this might be more fun for the exhibitor and especially for the novice. The U.S. is very handler-oriented in many of the breeds. It is true, in most instances, that the experienced professional handler can present the dog better and will have a feel for what a judge likes.

In England, Crufts is The Kennel Club's own show and is most assuredly the largest dog show in the world. They've been known to have an entry of nearly 20,000, and the show lasts four days. Entry is only gained by qualifying through winning in specified classes at another Championship Show. Westminster is strictly conformation, but Crufts exhibitors and spectators enjoy not only conformation but obedience, agility and a multitude of exhibitions as well. Obedience was admitted in 1957 and agility in 1983.

If you are handling your own dog, please give some consideration to your apparel. For sure the dress code at matches is more informal than the point shows. However, you should wear something a little more appropriate than beach attire or ragged jeans and bare feet. If you check out the handlers and see what is presently fashionable, you'll catch on. Men usually dress with a shirt and tie and a nice sports coat. Whether you are male or female, you will want to wear comfortable clothes and shoes. You need to be able to run with your dog and you certainly don't want to take a chance of falling and hurting yourself. Heaven forbid, if nothing else, you'll upset your dog. Women usually wear a dress or two-piece outfit, preferably with pockets to carry bait, comb, brush, etc. In this case men are the lucky ones with all their pockets. Ladies, think about where your dress will be if you need to kneel on the floor and also think about running. Does it allow freedom to do so?

You need to take along dog; crate; ex pen (if you use one); extra newspaper; water pail and water; all required grooming equipment, including hair dryer and extension cord; table; chair for you; bait for dog and lunch for you and friends; and, last but not least, clean up materials, such as plastic bags, paper towels, and perhaps a bath towel and some shampoo— just in case. Don't forget your entry confirmation and directions to the show.

If you are showing in obedience, then you will want to wear pants. Many of our top obedience handlers wear pants that are color-coordinated with their dogs. The philosophy is that imperfections in the black dog will be less obvious next to your black pants.

Whether you are showing in conformation, Junior Showmanship or obedience, you need to watch the clock and be sure you are not late. It is customary to pick up your conformation armband a few minutes before the start of the class. They will not wait for you and if you are on the show grounds and not in the ring, you will upset everyone. It's a little more complicated picking up your obedience armband if you show later in the class. If you have not picked up your armband and they get to your number, you may not be allowed to show. It's best to pick up your armband early, but then you may show earlier than expected if other handlers don't pick up. Customarily all conflicts should be discussed with the judge prior to the start of the class.

Life's not just a spectator sport! There are many activities that you and your Scottie can get involved in that will enrich both of your lives.

Junior Showmanship

The Junior Showmanship Class is a wonderful way to build self

confidence even if there are no aspirations of staying with the dog-show game later in life. Frequently, Junior Showmanship becomes the background of those who become successful exhibitors/handlers in the future. In some instances it is taken very seriously, and success is measured in terms of wins. The Junior Handler is judged solely on his ability and skill in presenting his dog. The dog's conformation is not to be considered by the judge. Even so the condition and grooming of the dog may be a reflection upon the handler.

Usually the matches and point shows include different classes. The Junior Handler's dog may be entered in a breed or obedience class and even shown by another person in that class. Junior Showmanship classes are usually divided by age and perhaps sex. The age is determined by the handler's age on the day of the show.

CANINE GOOD CITIZEN

The AKC sponsors a program to encourage dog owners to train their dogs. Local clubs perform the pass/fail tests, and dogs who pass are awarded a Canine Good Citizen Certificate. Proof of vaccination is required at the time of participation. The test includes:

1. Accepting a friendly stranger.
2. Sitting politely for petting.
3. Appearance and grooming.
4. Walking on a loose leash.
5. Walking through a crowd.
6. Sit and down on command/staying in place.
7. Come when called.
8. Reaction to another dog.
9. Reactions to distractions.
10. Supervised separation.

If more effort was made by pet owners to accomplish these exercises, fewer dogs would be cast off to the humane shelter.

OBEDIENCE

Obedience is necessary, without a doubt, but it can also become a wonderful hobby or even an obsession. Obedience classes and competition can provide wonderful companionship, not only with your dog but with your classmates or fellow competitors. It is always gratifying to discuss your dog's problems with others who have had similar experiences. The AKC acknowledged Obedience around 1936, and it has changed tremendously even though many of the exercises are basically the same. Today, obedience competition is just that—very competitive. Even so, it is possible for every obedience exhibitor to come home a winner (by earning qualifying scores) even though he/she may not earn a placement in the class.

Canine good citizens must be able to get along well with other animals. This Scottie looks as if he has passed the test!

Most of the obedience titles are awarded after earning three qualifying scores (legs) in the appropriate class under three different judges. These classes offer a perfect score of 200, which is extremely rare. Each of the class exercises has its own point value. A leg is earned after receiving a score of at least 170 and at least 50 percent of the points available in each exercise. The titles are:

Companion Dog—CD

This is called the Novice Class and the exercises are:

1.Heel on leash and figure 8	40 points
2.Stand for examination	30 points
3.Heel free	40 points
4.Recall	30 points
5.Long sit—one minute	30 points
6.Long down—three minutes	30 points
Maximum total score	200 points

Companion Dog Excellent—CDX

This is the Open Class and the exercises are:

1.Heel off leash and figure 8	40 points
2.Drop on recall	30 points
3.Retrieve on flat	20 points

4.Retrieve over high jump	30 points
5.Broad jump	20 points
6.Long sit—three minutes (out of sight)	30 points
7.Long down—five minutes (out of sight)	30 points
Maximum total score	200 points

Utility Dog—UD

The Utility Class exercises are:

1.Signal Exercise	40 points
2.Scent discrimination-Article 1	30 points
3.Scent discrimination-Article 2	30 points
4.Directed retrieve	30 points
5.Moving stand and examination	30 points
6.Directed jumping	40 points
Maximum total score	200 points

After achieving the UD title, you may feel inclined to go after the UDX and/or OTCh. The UDX (Utility Dog Excellent) title went into effect in January 1994. It is not easily attained. The title requires qualifying simultaneously ten times in Open B and Utility B but not necessarily at consecutive shows.

The OTCh (Obedience Trial Champion) is awarded after the dog has earned his UD and then goes on to earn 100 championship points, a first place in Utility, a first place in Open and another first place in either class. The placements must be won under three different judges at all-breed obedience trials. The points are determined by the number of dogs competing in the Open B and Utility B classes. The OTCh title precedes the dog's name.

Obedience matches (AKC Sanctioned, Fun, and Show and Go) are usually available. Usually they are sponsored by the local obedience clubs. When preparing an obedience dog for a title, you will find matches very helpful. Fun Matches and Show and Go Matches are more lenient in allowing you to make corrections in the ring. This type of training is usually very necessary for the Open and Utility Classes. AKC Sanctioned Obedience Matches do not allow corrections in the ring since they must abide by the AKC Obedience Regulations. If you are interested

Handlers must wear comfortable practical clothing that does not distract attention from the dog they are showing.

in showing in obedience, then you should contact the AKC for a copy of the Obedience Regulations.

AGILITY

Agility was first introduced by John Varley in England at the Crufts Dog Show, February 1978, but Peter Meanwell, competitor and judge, actually developed the idea. It was officially recognized in the early '80s. Agility is extremely popular in England and Canada and growing in popularity in the U.S. The AKC acknowledged agility in August 1994. Dogs must be at least 12 months of age to be entered. It is a fascinating sport that the dog, handler and spectators enjoy to the utmost. Agility is a spectator sport! The dog performs off lead. The handler either runs with his dog or positions himself on the course and directs his dog with verbal and hand signals over a timed course over or through a variety of obstacles including a time out or pause. One of the main drawbacks to agility is finding a place to train. The obstacles take up a lot of space and it is very time consuming to put up and take down courses.

The titles earned at AKC agility trials are Novice Agility Dog (NAD), Open Agility Dog (OAD), Agility Dog Excellent (ADX), and Master Agility Excellent (MAX). In order to acquire an agility title, a dog must earn a qualifying score in its respective class on three separate occasions under two different judges. The MAX will be awarded after earning ten qualifying scores in the Agility Excellent Class.

Agility is just one of the many activities in which Scottish Terriers can demonstrate their athletic and competitive prowess.

PERFORMANCE TESTS

During the last decade the American Kennel Club has promoted performance tests—those events that test the different breeds' natural abilities. This type of event encourages a handler to devote even more time to his dog and retain the natural instincts of his breed heritage. It is an important part of the wonderful world of dogs.

Scottish Terriers excel in scenting exercises because of their natural ability to use their noses.

GENERAL INFORMATION

Obedience, tracking and agility allow the purebred dog with an Indefinite Listing Privilege (ILP) number or a limited registration to be exhibited and earn titles. Application must be made to the AKC for an ILP number.

The American Kennel Club publishes a monthly *Events* magazine that is part of the *Gazette*, their official journal for the sport of purebred dogs. The *Events* section lists upcoming shows and the secretary or superintendent for them. The majority of the conformation shows in the U.S. are overseen by licensed superintendents. Generally the entry closing date is approximately two-and-a-half weeks before the actual show. Point shows are fairly expensive, while the match shows cost about one third of the point show entry fee. Match shows usually take entries the day of the show but some are pre-entry. The best way to find match show information is through your local kennel club. Upon asking, the AKC can provide you with a list of superintendents, and you can write and ask to be put on their mailing lists.

Obedience trial and tracking test information is available through the AKC. Frequently these events are not superintended, but put on by the host club. Therefore you would make the entry with the event's secretary.

As you have read, there are numerous activities you can share with your dog. Regardless what you do, it does take teamwork. Your dog can only benefit from your attention and training. We hope this chapter has enlightened you and hope, if nothing else, you will attend a show here and there. Perhaps you will start with a puppy kindergarten class, and who knows where it may lead!

HEALTH CARE

Veterinary medicine has become far more sophisticated than what was available to our ancestors. This can be attributed to the increase in household pets and consequently the demand for better care for them. Also human medicine has become far more complex. Today diagnostic testing in veterinary medicine parallels human diagnostics. Because of better technology we can expect our pets to live healthier lives thereby increasing their life spans.

For the sake of your puppy as well as the health of your family, you should bring your new Scottie to the veterinarian within three days of his arrival at your home.

THE FIRST CHECK UP

You will want to take your new puppy/dog in for its first check up within 48 to 72 hours after acquiring it. Many breeders strongly recommend this check up and so do the humane shelters. A puppy/dog can appear healthy but it may have a serious problem that is not apparent to the layman. Most pets have some type of a minor flaw that may never cause a real problem.

Unfortunately if he/she should have a serious problem, you will want to

All Scottish Terrier puppies are cute, but not all are of breeding quality. Reputable breeders will often sell pet-quality pups on the condition that they are spayed or neutered.

consider the consequences of keeping the pet and the attachments that will be formed, which may be broken prematurely. Keep in mind there are many healthy dogs looking for good homes.

This first check up is a good time to establish yourself with the veterinarian and learn the office policy regarding their hours and how they handle emergencies. Usually the breeder or another conscientious pet owner is a good reference for locating a capable veterinarian. You should be aware that not all veterinarians give the same quality of service. Please do not make your selection on the least expensive clinic, as they may be short changing your pet. There is the possibility that eventually it will cost you more due to improper diagnosis, treatment, etc. If you are selecting a new veterinarian, feel free to ask for a tour of the clinic. You should inquire about making an appointment for a tour since all clinics are working clinics, and therefore may not be available all day for sightseers. You may worry less if you see where your pet will be spending the day if he ever needs to be hospitalized.

THE PHYSICAL EXAM

Your veterinarian will check your pet's overall condition, which includes listening to the heart; checking the respiration; feeling the abdomen, muscles and joints; checking the mouth, which includes the gum color and signs of gum disease along with plaque buildup; checking the ears for signs of an infection or ear mites; examining the eyes; and, last but not least, checking the condition of the skin and coat.

He should ask you questions regarding your pet's eating and elimination habits and invite you to relay your questions. It is a good idea to prepare a list so as not to forget anything. He should discuss the proper diet and the quantity to be fed. If this should differ from your breeder's recommendation, then you should convey to him the breeder's choice and see if he approves. If he recommends changing the diet, then this should be done over a few days so as not to cause a gastrointestinal upset. It is customary to take in a fresh stool sample (just a small amount) for a test for intestinal parasites. It must be fresh, preferably within 12 hours, since the eggs hatch quickly and after hatching will not be observed under the microscope. If your pet isn't obliging then, usually the technician can take one in the clinic.

IMMUNIZATIONS

It is important that you take your puppy/dog's vaccination record with you on your first visit. In case of a puppy, presumably the breeder has seen to the vaccinations up to the

Scottish Terriers are active and playful. Any change in behavior should be brought to your veterinarian's attention immediately.

time you acquired custody. Veterinarians differ in their vaccination protocol. It is not unusual for your puppy to have received vaccinations for distemper, hepatitis, leptospirosis, parvovirus and parainfluenza every two to three weeks from the age of five or six weeks. Usually this is a combined injection and is typically called the

Regular medical care is extremely important to the young puppy. Vaccinations and physical exams are part of your Scottie's lifelong maintenance.

DHLPP. The DHLPP is given through at least 12 to 14 weeks of age, and it is customary to continue with another parvovirus vaccine at 16 to 18 weeks. You may wonder why so many immunizations are necessary. No one knows for sure when the puppy's maternal antibodies are gone, although it is customarily accepted that distemper antibodies are gone by 12 weeks. Usually parvovirus antibodies are gone by 16 to 18 weeks of age. However, it is possible for the maternal antibodies to be gone at a much earlier age or even a later age. Therefore immunizations are started at an early age. The vaccine will not give immunity as long as there are maternal antibodies.

The rabies vaccination is given at three or six months of age depending on your local laws. A vaccine for bordetella (kennel cough) is advisable and can be given anytime from the age of five weeks. The coronavirus is not commonly given unless there is a problem locally. The Lyme vaccine is necessary in endemic areas. Lyme disease has been reported in 47 states.

Distemper

This is virtually an incurable disease. If the dog recovers, he is subject to severe nervous disorders. The virus attacks every tissue in the body and resembles a bad cold with a fever. It can cause a runny nose and eyes and cause gastrointestinal disorders, including a poor appetite, vomiting and diarrhea. The virus is carried by raccoons, foxes, wolves, mink and other dogs. Unvaccinated youngsters and senior citizens are very susceptible. This is still a common disease.

Hepatitis

This is a virus that is most serious in very young dogs. It is spread by contact with an infected animal or its stool or urine. The virus affects the liver and kidneys and is characterized by high fever, depression and lack of appetite. Recovered animals may be afflicted with chronic illnesses.

Leptospirosis

This is a bacterial disease transmitted by contact with the urine of an infected dog, rat or other wildlife. It produces severe symptoms of fever, depression, jaundice and internal bleeding and was fatal before the vaccine was developed. Recovered dogs can be carriers, and the disease can be transmitted from dogs to humans.

Parvovirus

This was first noted in the late 1970s and is still a fatal disease. However, with proper vaccinations, early diagnosis and prompt treatment, it is a manageable disease. It attacks the bone marrow and intestinal tract. The symptoms include depression, loss of appetite, vomiting, diarrhea and collapse. Immediate medical attention is of the essence.

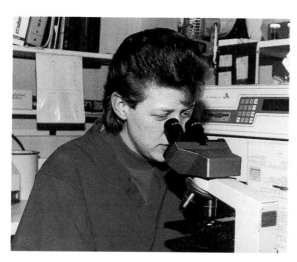

Laboratory tests are studied by highly trained veterinary technicians. Most tests are performed right in your own veterinarian's office.

Rabies

This is shed in the saliva and is carried by raccoons, skunks, foxes, other dogs and cats. It attacks nerve tissue, resulting in paralysis and death. Rabies can be transmitted to people and is virtually always fatal. This disease is reappearing in the suburbs.

Bordetella (Kennel Cough)

The symptoms are coughing, sneezing, hacking and retching accompanied by nasal discharge usually lasting from a few days to several weeks. There are several disease-producing organisms responsible for this disease. The present vaccines are helpful but do not protect for all the strains. It usually is not life threatening but in some instances it can progress to a serious bronchopneumonia. The disease is highly contagious. The vaccination should be given routinely for dogs that come in contact with other dogs, such as through boarding, training class or visits to the groomer.

Bordetella attached to canine cilia. Otherwise known as kennel cough, this disease is highly contagious and should be vaccinated against routinely.

Coronavirus

This is usually self limiting and not life threatening. It was first noted in the late '70s about a year before parvovirus. The virus produces a yellow/brown stool and there may be depression, vomiting and diarrhea.

Lyme Disease

This was first diagnosed in the United States in 1976 in Lyme, CT in people who lived in close proximity to the deer tick. Symptoms may include acute lameness, fever, swelling of joints and loss of appetite. Your veterinarian can advise you if you live in an endemic area.

After your puppy has completed his puppy vaccinations, you will continue to booster the DHLPP once a year. It is customary to booster the rabies one year after the first vaccine and then, depending on where you live, it should be boostered every year or every three years. This depends on your local laws. The Lyme and corona vaccines are boostered annually and it is recommended that the bordetella be boostered every six to eight months.

ANNUAL VISIT

I would like to impress the importance of the annual check up, which would include the booster vaccinations, check for intestinal parasites and test for heartworm. Today in our very busy world it is rush, rush and see "how much you can get for how little." Unbelievably, some non-veterinary businesses have entered into the vaccination business. More harm than good can come to your dog through improper vaccinations, possibly from inferior vaccines and/or the wrong schedule. More than likely you truly care about your companion dog and over the years you have devoted much time and expense to his well being. Perhaps you are unaware that a vaccination is not just a vaccination. There is more involved. Please, please follow through with regular physical examinations. It is so important for your veterinarian to know your dog and this is especially true during middle age through the geriatric years. More than likely your older dog will require more than one physical a year. The annual physical is good preventive medicine. Through early diagnosis and subsequent treatment your dog can maintain a longer and better quality of life.

The deer tick is the most common carrier of Lyme disease. Photo courtesy of Virbac Laboratories, Inc., Fort Worth, Texas.

INTESTINAL PARASITES

Hookworms

These are almost microscopic intestinal worms that can cause anemia and therefore serious problems, including death,

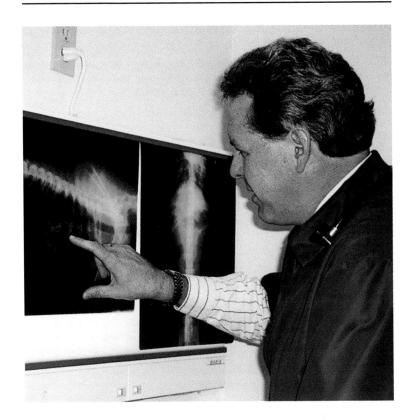

Regular visits to the veterinarian will help in the timely diagnosis of any illnesses or parasitic infections.

in young puppies. Hookworms can be transmitted to humans through penetration of the skin. Puppies may be born with them.

Roundworms

These are spaghetti-like worms that can cause a potbellied appearance and dull coat along with more severe symptoms, such as vomiting, diarrhea and coughing. Puppies acquire these while in the mother's uterus and through lactation. Both hookworms and roundworms may be acquired through ingestion.

Whipworms

These have a three-month life cycle and are not acquired through the dam. They cause intermittent diarrhea usually with mucus. Whipworms are possibly the most difficult worm to eradicate. Their eggs are very resistant to most environmental factors and can last for years until the proper conditions enable them to mature. Whipworms are seldom seen in the stool.

Intestinal parasites are more prevalent in some areas than others. Climate, soil and contamination are big factors contributing to the incidence of intestinal parasites. Eggs are passed in the stool, lay on the ground and then become infective in a certain number of days. Each of the above worms has a different life cycle. Your best chance of becoming and remaining worm-free is to always pooper-scoop your yard. A fenced-in yard keeps stray dogs out, which is certainly helpful.

I would recommend having a fecal examination on your dog twice a year or more often if there is a problem. If your dog has a positive fecal sample, then he will be given the appropriate medication and you will be asked to bring back another stool sample in a certain period of time (depending on the type of worm) and then be rewormed. This process goes on until he has at least two negative samples. The different types of worms require different medications. You will be wasting your money and doing your dog an injustice by buying over-the-counter medication without first consulting your veterinarian.

OTHER INTERNAL PARASITES

Coccidiosis and Giardiasis

These protozoal infections usually affect puppies, especially in places where large numbers of puppies are brought together. Older dogs may harbor these infections but do not

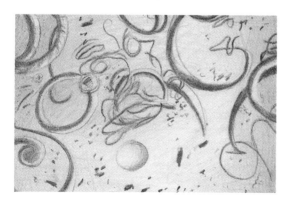

Whipworms are hard to find, and it is a job best left to a veterinarian. Pictured here are adult whipworms.

show signs unless they are stressed. Symptoms include diarrhea, weight loss and lack of appetite. These infections are not always apparent in the fecal examination.

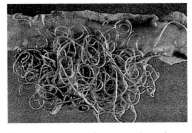

Tapeworms

Seldom apparent on fecal floatation, they are diagnosed frequently as rice-like segments around the dog's

When visiting the veterinarian, it is customary to take a stool sample to test for intestinal parasites, such as roundworms. Courtesy of Merck AgVet.

The cat flea is the most common flea of both dogs and cats. Courtesy of Fleabusters, RX for Fleas, Inc., Fort Lauderdale, Florida.

anus and the base of the tail. Tapeworms are long, flat and ribbon like, sometimes several feet in length, and made up of many segments about five-eighths of an inch long. The two most common types of tapeworms found in the dog are:

(1) First the larval form of the flea tapeworm parasite must mature in an intermediate host, the flea, before it can become infective. Your dog acquires this by ingesting the flea through licking and chewing.

(2) Rabbits, rodents and certain large game animals serve as intermediate hosts for other species of tapeworms. If your dog should eat one of these infected hosts, then he can acquire tapeworms.

HEARTWORM DISEASE

This is a worm that resides in the heart and adjacent blood vessels of the lung that produces microfilaria, which circulate in the bloodstream. It is possible for a dog to be infected with any number of worms from one to a hundred that can be 6 to 14 inches long. It is a life-threatening disease, expensive to treat and easily prevented. Depending on where you live, your veterinarian may recommend a preventive year-round and either an annual or semiannual blood test. The most common preventive is given once a month.

EXTERNAL PARASITES

Fleas

These pests are not only the dog's worst enemy but also enemy to the owner's pocketbook. Preventing is less expensive than treating, but regardless we'd prefer to spend our money elsewhere. Likely, the majority of our dogs are allergic to the bite of a flea, and in many cases it only takes one

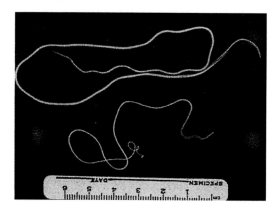

Tapeworms are long, flat, ribbon-like segmented parasites that often grow to several feet in length.

flea bite. The protein in the flea's saliva is the culprit. Allergic dogs have a reaction, which usually results in a "hot spot." More than likely such a reaction will involve a trip to the veterinarian for treatment. Yes, prevention is less expensive. Fortunately today there are several good products available.

If there is a flea infestation, no one product is going to correct the problem. Not only will the dog require treatment so will the environment. In general flea collars are not very

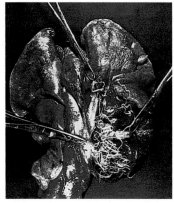

Dirofilaria—adult worms in the heart of a dog. Courtesy of Merck AgVet.

effective although there is now available an "egg" collar that will kill the eggs on the dog. Dips are the most economical but they are messy. There are some effective shampoos and treatments available through pet shops and veterinarians. An oral tablet arrived on the American market in 1995 and was popular in Europe the previous year. It sterilizes the female flea but will not kill adult fleas. Therefore the tablet, which is given monthly, will decrease the flea population but is not a "cure-all." Those dogs that suffer from flea-bite allergy will still be subjected to the bite of the flea. Another popular parasiticide is permethrin, which is applied to the back of the dog in one or two places depending on the dog's weight. This product works as a repellent causing the flea to get "hot feet" and jump off. Do not confuse this product with some of the organophosphates that are also applied to the dog's back.

Some products are not usable on young puppies. Treating fleas should be done under your veterinarian's guidance. Frequently it is necessary to combine products and the layman does not have the knowledge regarding possible toxicities. It is hard to believe but there are a few dogs that do have a natural resistance to fleas. Nevertheless it would be wise to treat all pets at the same time. Don't forget your cats. Cats just love to prowl the neighborhood and consequently return with unwanted guests.

Adult fleas live on the dog but their eggs drop off the dog into the environment. There they go through four larval stages before reaching adulthood, and thereby are able to jump back on the poor unsuspecting dog. The cycle resumes and takes between 21 to 28 days under ideal conditions. There are environmental products available that will kill both the adult fleas and the larvae.

Ticks

Ticks carry Rocky Mountain Spotted Fever, Lyme disease and can cause tick paralysis. They should be removed with tweezers, trying to pull out the head. The jaws carry disease. There is a tick preventive collar that does an excellent job. The ticks automatically back out on those dogs wearing collars.

Sarcoptic Mange

This is a mite that is difficult to find on skin scrapings. The pinnal reflex is a good indicator of this disease. Rub the ends of the pinna (ear) together and the dog will start scratching with his foot. Sarcoptes are highly contagious to other dogs and to humans although they do not live long on humans. They cause intense itching.

Demodectic Mange

This is a mite that is passed from the dam to her puppies. It affects youngsters age three to ten months. Diagnosis is confirmed by skin scraping. Small areas of alopecia around the eyes, lips and/or forelegs become visible. There is little itching unless there is a secondary bacterial infection. Some breeds are afflicted more than others.

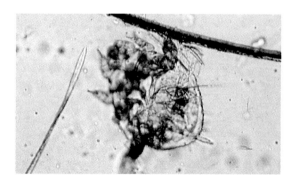

Sarcoptic mange is highly contagious to other dogs as well as humans. Sarcoptes cause intense itching.

Cheyletiella

This causes intense itching and is diagnosed by skin scraping. It lives in the outer layers of the skin of dogs, cats, rabbits and humans. Yellow-gray scales may be found on the back and the rump, top of the head and the nose.

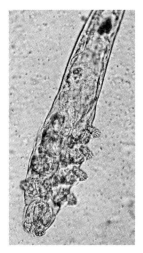

Demodectic mange is passed from a dam to her puppies. It involves areas of hair loss.

TO BREED OR NOT TO BREED

More than likely your breeder has requested that you have your puppy neutered or spayed. Your breeder's request is based on what is healthiest for your dog and what is most beneficial for your breed. Experienced and conscientious breeders devote many years into developing a bloodline. In order to do this, he makes every effort to plan each breeding in regard to conformation, temperament and health. This type of breeder does his best to perform the necessary testing (i.e., OFA, CERF, testing for inherited blood disorders, thyroid, etc.). Testing is expensive and sometimes very disheartening when a favorite dog doesn't pass his health tests. The health history pertains not only to the breeding stock but to the immediate ancestors. Reputable breeders do not want their offspring to be bred indiscriminately. Therefore you may be asked to neuter or spay your puppy. Of course there is always the exception, and your breeder may agree to let you breed your dog under his direct supervision. This is an important concept. More and more effort is being made to breed healthier dogs.

Spay/Neuter

There are numerous benefits of performing this surgery at six months of age. Unspayed females are subject to mammary and ovarian cancer. In order to prevent mammary cancer she must be spayed prior to her first heat cycle. Later in life, an unspayed female may develop a pyometra (an infected uterus), which is definitely life threatening.

Spaying is performed under a general anesthetic and is easy on the young dog. As you might expect it is a little harder on the older dog, but that is no reason to deny her the surgery. The surgery removes the ovaries and uterus. It is important to remove all the ovarian tissue. If some is left behind, she could remain attractive to males. In order to view the ovaries, a reasonably long incision is necessary. An ovariohysterectomy is considered major surgery.

Neutering the male at a young age will inhibit some characteristic male behavior that owners frown upon. Some boys will not hike their legs and mark territory if they are neutered at six months of age. Also neutering at a young age has hormonal benefits, lessening the chance of hormonal aggressiveness.

Breeding dogs of only the best quality ensures that good health and temperament are passed down to each new generation.

Surgery involves removing the testicles but leaving the scrotum. If there should be a retained testicle,

then he definitely needs to be neutered before the age of two or three years. Retained testicles can develop into cancer. Unneutered males are at risk for testicular cancer, perineal fistulas, perianal tumors and fistulas and prostatic disease.

Intact males and females are prone to housebreaking accidents. Females urinate frequently before, during and after heat cycles, and males tend to mark territory if there is a female in heat. Males may show the same behavior if there is a visiting dog or guests.

Surgery involves a sterile operating procedure equivalent to human surgery. The incision site is shaved, surgically scrubbed and draped. The veterinarian wears a sterile surgical gown, cap, mask and gloves. Anesthesia should be monitored by a

Breeding should be attempted only by someone who is conscientious, knowledgeable, and willing to take responsibility for the dogs and new puppies involved.

registered technician. It is customary for the veterinarian to recommend a pre-anesthetic blood screening, looking for metabolic problems and a ECG rhythm strip to check for normal heart function. Today anesthetics are equal to human anesthetics, which enables your dog to walk out of the clinic the same day as surgery.

Some folks worry about their dog gaining weight after being neutered or spayed. This is usually not the case. It is true that some dogs may be less active so they could develop a problem, but most dogs are just as active as they were before surgery. However, if your dog should begin to gain, then you need to decrease his food and see to it that he gets a little more exercise.

DENTAL CARE for Your Dog's Life

So you've got a new puppy! You also have a new set of puppy teeth in your household. Anyone who has ever raised a puppy is abundantly aware of these new teeth. Your puppy will chew anything it can reach, chase your shoelaces, and play "tear the rag" with any piece of clothing it can find. When puppies are newly born, they have no teeth. At about four weeks of age, puppies of most breeds begin to develop their deciduous or baby teeth. They begin eating semi-solid food, fighting and biting with their litter mates, and learning discipline from their mother. As their new teeth come in, they inflict more pain on their mother's breasts, so her feeding sessions become less frequent and shorter. By six or eight weeks, the mother will start growling to warn her pups when they are fighting too roughly or hurting her as they nurse too much with their new teeth.

Puppies need to chew. It is a necessary part of their physical and mental development. They develop muscles and necessary life skills as they drag objects around, fight over possession, and vocalize alerts and warnings. Puppies chew on things to explore their world. They are using their sense of taste to determine what is food and what is not. How else can they tell an electrical cord from a lizard? At about four months of age, most puppies begin shedding their baby teeth. Often these teeth need some help to come out and make way for the permanent teeth. The incisors (front teeth) will be replaced first. Then, the adult canine or fang teeth erupt. When the baby tooth is not shed before the permanent tooth comes in, veterinarians call it a retained deciduous tooth. This condition will often cause gum infections by trapping hair and debris between the permanent tooth and the retained baby tooth. Nylafloss® is an excellent device for puppies to use. They can toss it, drag it, and chew on the many surfaces it presents. The baby teeth can catch in the nylon material, aiding in their removal. Puppies that have adequate chew toys will have less destructive behavior, develop more physically, and have less chance of retained deciduous teeth.

During the first year, your dog should be seen by your veterinarian at regular intervals. Your veterinarian will let you know when to bring in your puppy for vaccinations and parasite examinations. At each visit, your veterinarian should inspect the lips, teeth, and mouth as part of a complete physical examination. You should take some part in the maintenance of your dog's oral health. You should examine your dog's mouth weekly throughout his first year to make sure there are no sores, foreign objects, tooth problems, etc. If your dog drools excessively, shakes its head, or has bad breath, consult your veterinarian. By the time your dog is six months old, the permanent teeth are all in and plaque can start to accumulate on the tooth surfaces. This is when your dog needs to develop good dental-care habits to prevent calculus build-up on its teeth. Brushing is best. That is a fact that cannot be denied. However, some dogs do not like their teeth brushed regularly, or you may not be able to accomplish the task. In that case, you should consider a product that will help prevent plaque and calculus build-up.

There is only one material suitable for flossing human teeth and that's nylon. So why not get a chew toy that will enable you to interact with your Scottish Terrier while it promotes dental health? As you play tug-of-war with a Nylafloss™, you'll be slowly pulling the nylon strand through your dog's teeth.

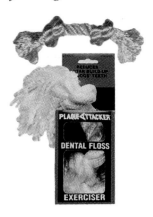

The Plaque Attackers® and Galileo Bone® are other excellent choices for the first three years of a dog's life. Their shapes make them interesting for the dog. As the dog chews on them, the solid polyurethane massages the gums which improves the blood circulation to the periodontal tissues. Projections on the chew devices increase the surface and are in contact with the tooth for more efficient cleaning. The unique shape and consistency prevent your dog from exerting excessive force on his own teeth or from breaking off pieces of the bone. If your dog is an aggressive chewer or weighs more than 55 pounds (25 kg), you should consider giving him a Nylabone®, the most durable chew product on the market.

The Gumabones®, made by the Nylabone Company, is constructed of strong polyurethane, which is softer than nylon. Less powerful chewers prefer the Gumabones® to the Nylabones®. A super option for your dog is the Hercules Bone®, a uniquely shaped bone named after the great Olympian for its exception strength. Like all Nylabone products, they are specially scented to make them attractive to your dog. Ask your veterinarian about these bones and he will validate the good doctor's prescription: Nylabones® not only give your dog a good chewing workout but also help to save your dog's teeth (and even his life, as it protects him from possible fatal periodontal diseases).

By the time dogs are four years old, 75% of them have periodontal disease. It is the most common infection in dogs. Yearly examinations by your veterinarian are essential to maintaining your dog's good health. If your veterinarian detects periodontal disease, he or she may recommend a prophylactic cleaning. To do a thorough cleaning, it will be necessary to put your dog under anesthesia. With modern gas anesthetics and monitoring equipment, the procedure is pretty safe. Your veterinarian will scale the teeth with an ultrasound scaler or hand instrument. This removes the calculus from the teeth. If there are calculus deposits below the gum line, the veterinarian will plane the roots to make them smooth. After all of the calculus has been removed, the teeth are polished with pumice in a polishing cup. If any medical or surgical treatment is needed, it is done at this time. The final step would be fluoride treatment and your follow-up treatment at home. If the periodontal disease is advanced, the veterinarian may prescribe a medicated mouth rinse or antibiotics for use at home. Make sure your dog has safe, clean and attractive chew toys and treats. Chooz® treats are another way

Raised dental tips on the surface of every Plaque Attacker™ bone help to combat plaque and tartar. Safe for aggressive chewers and ruggedly constructed to last, Plaque Attacker™ dental bones provide hours and hours of tooth-saving enjoyment.

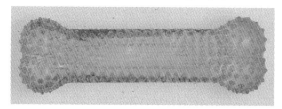

of using a consumable treat to help keep your dog's teeth clean.

Rawhide is the most popular of all materials for a dog to chew. This has never been good news to dog owners, because rawhide is inherently very dangerous for dogs. Thousands of dogs have died from rawhide, having swallowed the hide after it has become soft and mushy, only to cause stomach and intestinal blockage. A new rawhide product on the market has finally solved the problem of rawhide: molded Roar-Hide® from Nylabone. These are composed of processed, cut up, and melted American rawhide injected into your dog's favorite shape: a dog bone. These dog-safe devices smell and taste like rawhide but don't break up. The ridges on the bones help to fight tartar build-up on the teeth and they last ten times longer than the usual rawhide chews.

Brushing your dog's teeth is recommended by every veterinarian. Use the 2-Brush™ regularly, 3-4 times per week, and you may never need your veterinarian to do the job for you.

As your dog ages, professional examination and cleaning should become more frequent. The mouth should be inspected at least once a year. Your veterinarian may recommend visits every six months. In the geriatric patient, organs such as the heart, liver, and kidneys do not function as well as when they were young. Your veterinarian will probably want to test these organs' functions prior to using general anesthesia for dental cleaning. If your dog is a good chewer and you work closely with your veterinarian, your dog can keep all of its teeth all of its life. However, as your dog ages, his sense of smell, sight, and taste will diminish. He may not have the desire to chase, trap or chew his toys. He will also not have the energy to chew for long periods, as arthritis and periodontal disease make chewing painful. This will leave you with more responsibility for keeping his teeth clean and healthy. The dog that would not let you brush his teeth at one year of age, may let you brush his teeth now that he is ten years old.

If you train your dog with good chewing habits as a puppy, he will have healthier teeth throughout his life.

TRAVELING with Your Dog

The earlier you start traveling with your new puppy or dog, the better. He needs to become accustomed to traveling. However, some dogs are nervous riders and become carsick easily. It is helpful if he starts with an empty stomach. Do not despair, as it will go better if you continue taking him with you on short fun rides. How would you feel if every time you rode in the car you stopped at the doctor's for an injection? You would soon dread that nasty car. Older dogs that tend to get carsick may have more of a problem adjusting to traveling. Those dogs that are having a serious problem may benefit from some medication prescribed by the veterinarian.

The earlier you take your Scottish Terrier traveling with you, the quicker he will become accustomed to riding in a car.

Do give your dog a chance to relieve himself before getting into the car. It is a good idea to be prepared for a clean up with a leash, paper towels, bag and terry cloth towel.

The safest place for your dog is in a fiberglass crate, although close confinement can promote carsickness in some dogs. If your dog is nervous you can try letting him ride on the seat next to you or in someone's lap.

An alternative to the crate would be to use a car harness made for dogs and/or a safety strap attached to the harness or collar. Whatever you do, do not let your dog ride in the back of a pickup truck unless he is securely tied on a very short lead. I've seen trucks stop quickly and, even though the dog was tied, it fell out and was dragged.

Before any car excursion, be sure your Scottie is allowed plenty of time outdoors to attend to his needs.

Another advantage of the crate is that it is a safe place to leave him if you need to run into the store. Otherwise you wouldn't be able to leave the windows down. Keep in mind that while many dogs are overly protective in their crates, this may not be enough to deter dognappers. In some states it is against the law to leave a dog in the car unattended.

Never leave a dog loose in the car wearing a collar and leash. More than one dog has killed himself by hanging. Do not let him put his head out an open window. Foreign debris can be blown into his eyes. When leaving your dog unattended in a car, consider the temperature. It can take less than five minutes to reach temperatures over 100 degrees Fahrenheit.

TRIPS

Perhaps you are taking a trip. Give consideration to what is best for your dog—traveling with you or boarding. When traveling by car, van or motor home, you need to think ahead about locking your vehicle. In all probability you have many

Crates are a safe way for your dog to travel. The fiberglass crates are the safest for air travel, but the metal crates allow for better air circulation.

valuables in the car and do not wish to leave it unlocked. Perhaps most valuable and not replaceable is your dog. Give thought to securing your vehicle and providing adequate ventilation for him. Another consideration for you when traveling with your dog is medical problems that may arise and little inconveniences, such as exposure to external parasites. Some areas of the country are quite flea infested. You may want to carry flea spray with you. This is even a good idea when staying in motels. Quite possibly you are not the only occupant of the room.

Unbelievably many motels and even hotels do allow canine guests, even some very first-class ones. Gaines Pet Foods Corporation publishes *Touring With Towser*, a directory of domestic hotels and motels that accommodate guests with dogs. Their address is Gaines TWT, PO Box 5700, Kankakee, IL, 60902. Call ahead to any motel that you may be considering and see if they accept pets. Sometimes it is necessary to pay a deposit against room damage. The management may feel reassured if you mention that your dog will be crated. If you do travel with your dog, take along plenty of baggies so that you can clean up after him. When we all do our share in cleaning up, we make it possible for motels to continue accepting our pets. As a matter of fact, you should practice cleaning up everywhere you take your dog.

Depending on where your are traveling, you may need an up-to-date health certificate issued by your veterinarian. It is good policy to take along your dog's medical information, which would include the name, address and phone number of your veterinarian, vaccination record, rabies certificate, and any medication he is taking.

AIR TRAVEL

When traveling by air, you need to contact the airlines to check their policy. Usually you have to make arrangements up to a couple of weeks in advance for traveling with your dog. The airlines require your dog to travel in an airline

A reputable boarding kennel will require that dogs receive the vaccination for kennel cough no less than two weeks before their scheduled stay.

approved fiberglass crate. Usually these can be purchased through the airlines but they are also readily available

in most pet-supply stores. If your dog is not accustomed to a crate, then it is a good idea to get him acclimated to it before your trip. The day of the actual trip you should withhold water about one hour ahead of departure and no food for about 12 hours. The airlines generally have temperature restrictions, which do not allow pets to travel if it is either too cold or too hot. Frequently these restrictions are based on the temperatures at the departure and arrival airports. It's best to inquire about a health certificate. These usually need to be issued within ten days of departure. You should arrange for non-stop, direct flights and if a commuter plane should be involved, check to see if it will carry dogs. Some don't. The Humane Society of the United States has put together a tip sheet for airline traveling. You can receive a copy by sending a self-addressed stamped envelope to:

The Humane Society of the United States
Tip Sheet
2100 L Street NW
Washington, DC 20037.

Regulations differ for traveling outside of the country and are sometimes changed without notice. Well in advance you need to write or call the appropriate consulate or agricultural department for instructions. Some countries have lengthy quarantines (six months), and countries differ in their rabies vaccination requirements. For instance, it may have to be given at least 30 days ahead of your departure.

Do make sure your dog is wearing proper identification including your name, phone number and city. You never know when you might be in an accident and separated from your dog. Or your dog could be frightened and somehow manage to escape and run away.

Another suggestion would be to carry in-case-of-emergency instructions. These would include the address and phone number of a relative or friend, your veterinarian's name, address and phone number, and your dog's medical information.

BOARDING KENNELS

Perhaps you have decided that you need to board your dog. Your veterinarian can recommend a good boarding facility or possibly a pet sitter that will come to your house. It is customary for the boarding kennel to ask for proof of vaccination for the DHLPP, rabies and bordetella vaccine. The bordetella should have been given within six months of boarding. This is for your protection. If they do not ask for this proof I would not board at their kennel. Ask about flea control. Those dogs that suffer flea-bite allergy can get in trouble at a boarding kennel. Unfortunately boarding kennels are limited on how much they are able to do.

For more information on pet sitting, contact NAPPS:
National Association of Professional Pet Sitters
1200 G Street, NW
Suite 760
Washington, DC 20005.
Some pet clinics have technicians that pet sit and technicians that board clinic patients in their homes. This may be an alternative for you. Ask your veterinarian if they have an employee that can help you. There is a definite advantage of having a technician care for your dog, especially if your dog is on medication or is a senior citizen.

If your Scottish Terrier is more comfortable at home when you travel, there may be reputable pet-sitting services available in your area.

You can write for a copy of *Traveling With Your Pet* from ASPCA, Education Department, 441 E. 92nd Street, New York, NY 10128.

IDENTIFICATION and Finding the Lost Dog

There are several ways of identifying your dog. The old standby is a collar with dog license, rabies, and ID tags. Unfortunately collars have a way of being separated from the dog and tags fall off. We're not suggesting you shouldn't use a collar and tags. If they stay intact and on the dog, they are the quickest way of identification.

For several years owners have been tattooing their dogs. Some tattoos use a number with a registry. Here lies the problem because there are several registries to check. If you wish to tattoo, use your social security number. The humane shelters have the means to trace it. It is usually done on the inside of the rear thigh. The area is first shaved and numbed. There is no pain, although a few dogs do not like the buzzing sound. Occasionally tattooing is not legible and needs to be redone.

The newest method of identification is microchipping. The microchip is no bigger than a grain of rice.

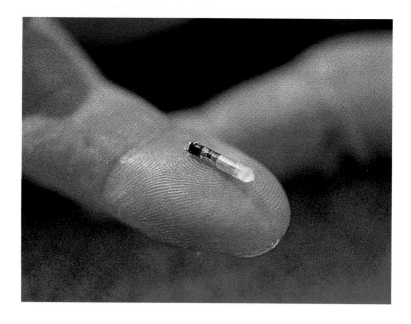

Scotties are easygoing dogs and enjoy accompanying their owners everywhere. These two eagerly await their next adventure.

The newest method of identification is microchipping. The microchip is a computer chip that is no larger than a grain of rice. The veterinarian implants it by injection between the shoulder blades. The dog feels no discomfort. If your dog is lost and picked up by the humane society, they can trace you by scanning the microchip, which has its own code. Microchip scanners are friendly to other brands of microchips and their registries. The microchip comes with a dog tag saying the dog is microchipped. It is the safest way of identifying your dog.

FINDING THE LOST DOG

I am sure you will agree that there would be little worse than losing your dog. Responsible pet owners rarely lose their dogs. They do not let their dogs run free because they don't want harm to come to them. Not only that but in most, if not all, states there is a leash law.

Beware of fenced-in yards. They can be a hazard. Dogs find ways to escape either over or under the fence. Another fast exit is through the gate that perhaps the neighbor's child left unlocked.

Below is a list that hopefully will be of help to you if you need it. Remember don't give up, keep looking. Your dog is worth your efforts.

Once your puppy is old enough for outdoor playtime make sure he wears a collar with tags at all times.

1. Contact your neighbors and put flyers with a photo on it in their mailboxes. Information you should include would be the dog's name, breed, sex, color, age, source of identification, when your dog was last seen and where, and your name and phone numbers. It may be helpful to say the dog needs medical care. Offer a *reward*.

2. Check all local shelters daily. It is also possible for your dog to be picked up away from home and end up in an out-of-the-way shelter. Check these too. Go in person. It is not good enough to call. Most shelters are limited on the time they can hold dogs then they are put up for adoption or euthanized. There is the possibility that your dog will not make it to the shelter for several days. Your dog could have been wandering or someone may have tried to keep him.

3. Notify all local veterinarians. Call and send flyers.

4. Call your breeder. Frequently breeders are contacted when one of their breed is found.

5. Contact the rescue group for your breed.

6. Contact local schools—children may have seen your dog.

Make sure you have a clear recent picture of your Scottie to distribute in case he becomes lost.

7. Post flyers at the schools, groceries, gas stations, convenience stores, veterinary clinics, groomers and any other place that will allow them.

8. Advertise in the newspaper.

9. Advertise on the radio.

BEHAVIOR and Canine Communication

S tudies of the human/animal bond point out the importance of the unique relationships that exist between people and their pets. Those of us who share our lives with pets understand the special part they play through companionship, service and protection. For many, the pet/owner bond goes beyond simple companionship; pets are often considered members of the family. A leading pet food manufacturer recently conducted a nationwide survey of pet owners to gauge just how important pets were in their lives. Here's what they found:

- 76 percent allow their pets to sleep on their beds
- 78 percent think of their pets as their children
- 84 percent display photos of their pets, mostly in their homes
- 84 percent think that their pets react to their own emotions
- 100 percent talk to their pets
- 97 percent think that their pets understand what they're saying

Dogs are a very important part of their owners lives, and the bond between humans and animals is a strong one.

Although some traits are inherited within a breed, every Scottish Terrier is an individual. These Scottish Terrier elves look like they agree!

Are you surprised?

Senior citizens show more concern for their own eating habits when they have the responsibility of feeding a dog. Seeing that their dog is routinely exercised encourages the owner to think of schedules that otherwise may seem unimportant to the senior citizen. The older owner may be arthritic and feeling poorly but with responsibility for his dog he has a reason to get up and get moving. It is a big plus if his dog is an attention seeker who will demand such from his owner.

Over the last couple of decades, it has been shown that pets relieve the stress of those who lead busy lives. Owning a pet has been known to lessen the occurrence of heart attack and stroke.

Many single folks thrive on the companionship of a dog. Lifestyles are very different from a long time ago, and today more individuals seek the single life. However, they receive fulfillment from owning a dog.

Most likely the majority of our dogs live in family environments. The companionship they provide is well worth the effort involved. In my opinion, every child should have the opportunity to have a family dog. Dogs teach responsibility through understanding their care, feelings and even respecting their life cycles. Frequently those children who have not been exposed to dogs grow up afraid of dogs, which isn't good. Dogs sense timidity and some will take advantage of the situation.

Today more dogs are serving as service dogs. Since the origination of the Seeing Eye dogs years ago, we now have trained hearing dogs. Also dogs are trained to provide service for the handicapped and are able to perform many different tasks for their owners. Search and Rescue dogs, with their handlers, are sent throughout the world to assist in recovery of disaster victims. They are life savers.

Therapy dogs are very popular with nursing homes, and some hospitals even allow them to visit. The inhabitants truly look forward to their visits. They wanted and were allowed to have visiting dogs in their beds to hold and love.

Nationally there is a Pet Awareness Week to educate students and others about the value and basic care of our pets. Many countries take an even greater interest in their pets than Americans do. In those countries the pets are allowed to accompany their owners into restaurants and shops, etc. In the U.S. this freedom is only available to our service dogs. Even so we think very highly of the human/animal bond.

CANINE BEHAVIOR

Canine behavior problems are the number-one reason for pet owners to dispose of their dogs, either through new homes, humane shelters or euthanasia. Unfortunately there are too many owners who are unwilling to devote the necessary time to properly train their dogs. On the other hand, there are those who not only are concerned about inherited health problems but are also aware of the dog's mental stability.

You may realize that a breed and his group relatives (i.e., sporting, hounds, etc.) show tendencies to behavioral characteristics. An experienced breeder can acquaint you with his breed's personality. Unfortunately many breeds are labeled with poor temperaments when actually the breed as a whole is not affected but only a small percentage of individuals within the breed.

Inheritance and environment contribute to the dog's behavior. Some naïve people suggest inbreeding as the cause of bad temperaments. Inbreeding only results in poor behavior if the ancestors carry the trait. If there are excellent temperaments behind the dogs, then inbreeding will promote good temperaments in the offspring. Did you ever consider that inbreeding is what sets the characteristics of a breed? A purebred dog is the end result of inbreeding. This does not spare the mixed-breed dog from the same problems. Mixed-breed dogs frequently are the offspring of purebred dogs.

Not too many decades ago most of our dogs led a different lifestyle than what is prevalent today. Usually mom stayed home so the dog had human companionship and someone to discipline it if needed. Not much was expected from the dog. Today's mom works and everyone's life is at a much faster pace.

The Galileo™ is the toughest nylon bone ever made. It is flavored to appeal to your Scottish Terrier and has a relatively soft outer layer. It is a necessary chew toy and doggy pacifier.

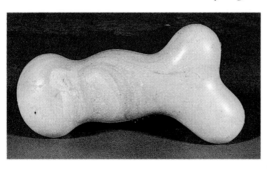

The dog may have to adjust to being a "weekend" dog. The family is gone all day during the week, and the dog is left to his own devices for entertainment. Some dogs sleep all day waiting for their family to come home and others become wigwam wreckers if given the opportunity. Crates do ensure the safety of the dog and the house. However, he could become a physically and emotionally cripple if he doesn't get enough exercise and attention. We still appreciate and want the companionship of our dogs although we expect more from them. In many cases we tend to forget dogs are just that—*dogs* not human beings.

SOCIALIZING AND TRAINING

Many prospective puppy buyers lack experience regarding the proper socialization and training needed to develop the type of pet we all desire. In the first 18 months, training does take some work. It is easier to start proper training before there is a problem that needs to be corrected.

The initial work begins with the breeder. The breeder should start socializing the puppy at five to six weeks of age and cannot let up. Human socializing is critical up through 12 weeks of age and likewise important during the following months. The litter should be left together during the first few weeks but it is necessary to separate them by ten weeks of age. Leaving them together after that time will increase competition for litter dominance. If puppies are not socialized with people by 12 weeks of age, they will be timid in later life.

The eight- to ten-week age period is a fearful time for puppies. They need to be handled very gently around children and adults. There should be no harsh discipline during this time. Starting at 14 weeks of age, the puppy begins the juvenile period, which ends when he reaches sexual

A properly socialized Scottie will be able to get along with all the members of a household. "McGregor" and his friend "Ignacio," owned by Dawn and Joel Bates, enjoy a day at the beach.

maturity around six to 14 months of age. During the juvenile period he needs to be introduced to strangers (adults, children and other dogs) on the home property. At sexual maturity he will begin to bark at strangers and become more protective. Males start to lift their legs to urinate but if you desire you can inhibit this behavior by walking your boy on leash away from trees, shrubs, fences, etc.

Perhaps you are thinking about an older puppy. You need to inquire about the puppy's social experience. If he has lived in a kennel, he may have a hard time adjusting to people and environmental stimuli. Assuming he has had a good social upbringing, there are advantages to an older puppy.

Training includes puppy kindergarten and a minimum of one to two basic training classes. During these classes you will learn how to dominate your youngster. This is especially important if you own a large breed of dog. It is somewhat harder, if not nearly impossible, for some owners to be the Alpha figure when their dog towers over them. You will be taught how to properly restrain your dog. This concept is important. Again it puts you in the Alpha position. All dogs need to be restrained

If you allow your Scottish Terrier to develop bad habits, like lying on the furniture, it can be very hard to break him of it later.

many times during their lives. Believe it or not, some of our worst offenders are the eight-week-old puppies that are brought to our clinic. They need to be gently restrained for a nail trim but the way they carry on you would think we were killing them. In comparison, their vaccination is a "piece of cake." When we ask dogs to do something that is not agreeable to them, then their worst comes out. Life will be easier for your dog if you expose him at a young age to the necessities of life—proper behavior and restraint.

Understanding the Dog's Language

Most authorities agree that the dog is a descendent of the wolf. The dog and wolf have similar traits. For instance both are pack oriented and prefer not to be isolated for long periods of time. Another characteristic is that the dog, like the wolf, looks to the leader–Alpha–for direction. Both the wolf and the dog communicate through body language, not only within their pack but with outsiders.

Every pack has an Alpha figure. The dog looks to you, or should look to you, to be that leader. If your dog doesn't receive the proper training and guidance, he very well may replace you as Alpha. This would be a serious problem and is certainly a disservice to your dog.

Eye contact is one way the Alpha wolf keeps order within his pack. You are Alpha so you must establish eye contact with your puppy. Obviously your puppy will have to look at you. Practice eye contact even if you need to hold his head for five to ten seconds at a time. You can give him a treat as a reward. Make sure your eye contact is gentle and not threatening. Later, if he has been naughty, it is permissible to give him a long, penetrating look. There are some older dogs that never learned eye contact as puppies and cannot accept eye contact. You should avoid eye contact with these dogs since they feel threatened and will retaliate as such.

BODY LANGUAGE

The play bow, when the forequarters are down and the hindquarters are elevated, is an invitation to play. Puppies play fight,

Scotties possess innate curiosity and can wander into all sorts of predicaments. Be sure to supervise your puppy at all times.

Your puppy's relationship with his littermates is an essential one. He will learn to interact with other dogs by playing with his siblings. which helps them learn the acceptable limits of biting. This is necessary for later in their lives. Nevertheless, an owner may be falsely reassured by the playful nature of his dog's aggression. Playful aggression toward another dog or human may be an indication of serious aggression in the future. Owners should never play fight or play tug-of-war with any dog that is inclined to be dominant.

Signs of submission are:

1. Avoids eye contact.
2. Active submission—the dog crouches down, ears back and the tail is lowered.
3. Passive submission—the dog rolls on his side with his hindlegs in the air and frequently urinates.

Signs of dominance are:

1. Makes eye contact.
2. Stands with ears up, tail up and the hair raised on his neck.
3. Shows dominance over another dog by standing at right angles over it.

Dominant dogs tend to behave in characteristic ways such as:

1. The dog may be unwilling to move from his place (i.e., reluctant to give up the sofa if the owner wants to sit there).
2. He may not part with toys or objects in his mouth and may show possessiveness with his food bowl.
3. He may not respond quickly to commands.
4. He may be disagreeable for grooming and dislikes to be petted.

Dogs are popular because of their sociable nature. Those that have contact with humans during the first 12 weeks of life regard them as a member of their own species—their pack. All dogs have the potential for both dominant and submissive behavior. Only through experience and training do they learn to whom it is appropriate to show which behavior. Not all dogs are concerned with dominance but owners need to be aware of that potential. It is wise for the owner to establish his dominance early on.

A human can express dominance or submission toward a dog in the following ways:

1. Meeting the dog's gaze signals dominance.

An unwillingness to give up his toys may signal that your dog is displaying dominant tendencies. Your Scottie must always know you are the boss.

Eye contact is an extremely important aspect of your relationship with your Scottish Terrier. It will help to establish you as pack leader in your dog's mind.

Averting the gaze signals submission. If the dog growls or threatens, averting the gaze is the first avoiding action to take—it may prevent attack. It is important to establish eye contact in the puppy. The older dog that has not been exposed to eye contact may see it as a threat and will not be willing to submit.

2. Being taller than the dog signals dominance; being lower signals submission. This is why, when attempting to make friends with a strange dog or catch the runaway, one should kneel down to his level. Some owners see their dogs become dominant when allowed on the furniture or on the bed. Then he is at the owner's level.

3. An owner can gain dominance by ignoring all the dog's

A puppy should not be forced into a situation he finds frightening. Respect his feelings and allow him to acclimate to the situation.

social initiatives. The owner pays attention to the dog only when he obeys a command.

No dog should be allowed to achieve dominant status over any adult or child. Ways of preventing are as follows:

1. Handle the puppy gently, especially during the three- to four-month period.
2. Let the children and adults handfeed him and teach him to take food without lunging or grabbing.
3. Do not allow him to chase children or joggers.
4. Do not allow him to jump on people or mount their legs. Even females may be inclined to mount. It is not only a male habit.
5. Do not allow him to growl for any reason.

6. Don't participate in wrestling or tug-of-war games.
7. Don't physically punish puppies for aggressive behavior. Restrain him from repeating the infraction and teach an alternative behavior. Dogs should earn everything they receive from their owners. This would include sitting to receive petting or treats, sitting before going out the door and sitting to receive the collar and leash. These types of exercises reinforce the owner's dominance.

Young children should never be left alone with a dog. It is important that children learn some basic obedience commands so they have some control over the dog. They will gain the respect of their dog.

Fear

One of the most common problems dogs experience is being fearful. Some dogs are more afraid than others. On the lesser side, which is sometimes humorous to watch, dogs can be afraid of a strange object. They act silly when something is out of place in the house. We call his problem perceptive intelligence. He realizes the abnormal within his known environment. He does not react the same way in strange environments since he does not know what is normal.

On the more serious side is a fear of people. This can result in backing off, seeking his own space and saying "leave me alone" or it can result in an aggressive behavior that may lead to challenging the person. Respect that the dog wants to be left alone and give him time to come forward. If you approach

There are all kinds of flying disks for dogs, but only one is made with strength, scent, and originality. The Nylabone® Frisbee™* is a must if you want to have this sort of fun with your Scottish Terrier. *The trademark Frisbee is used under license from Mattel, Inc., California, USA.

the cornered dog, he may resort to snapping. If you leave him alone, he may decide to come forward, which should be rewarded with a treat.

Some dogs may initially be too fearful to take treats. In these cases it is helpful to make sure the dog hasn't eaten for about 24 hours. Being a little hungry encourages him to accept the treats, especially if they are of the "gourmet" variety.

It is important to remember that your Scottish Terrier wants to please you and with patience will learn what you have to teach him.

Dogs can be afraid of numerous things, including loud noises and thunderstorms. Invariably the owner rewards (by comforting) the dog when it shows signs of fearfulness. When your dog is frightened, direct his attention to something else and act happy. Don't dwell on his fright.

AGGRESSION

Some different types of aggression are: predatory, defensive, dominance, possessive, protective, fear induced, noise provoked, "rage" syndrome (unprovoked aggression), maternal and aggression directed toward other dogs. Aggression is the most common behavioral problem encountered. Protective breeds are expected to be more aggressive than others but with the proper upbringing they can make very dependable companions. You need to be able to read your dog.

Many factors contribute to aggression including genetics and environment. An improper environment, which may include the living conditions, lack of social life, excessive punishment, being attacked or frightened by an aggressive dog, etc., can all influence a dog's

Scottie puppies are full of mischief. Although correction will sometimes be necessary, it will all prove worthwhile in the end.

behavior. Even spoiling him and giving too much praise may be detrimental. Isolation and the lack of human contact or exposure to frequent teasing by children or adults also can ruin a good dog.

Lack of direction, fear, or confusion lead to aggression in those dogs that are so inclined. Any obedience exercise, even the sit and down, can direct the dog and overcome fear and/or confusion. Every dog should learn these commands as a youngster, and there should be periodic reinforcement.

When a dog is showing signs of aggression, you should speak calmly (no screaming or hysterics) and firmly give a command that he understands, such as the sit. As soon as your dog obeys, you have assumed your dominant position. Aggression presents a problem because there may be danger to others. Sometimes it is an emotional issue. Owners may consciously or unconsciously encourage their dog's aggression. Other owners show responsibility by accepting the problem and taking measures to keep it under control. The owner is responsible for his dog's actions, and it is not wise to take a chance on someone being bitten, especially a child. Euthanasia is the solution for some owners and in severe cases this may be the best choice. However, few dogs are that dangerous and very few are that much of a threat to their owners. If caution is exercised and professional help is gained early on, most cases can be controlled.

Some authorities recommend feeding a lower protein (less than 20 percent) diet. They believe this can aid in reducing aggression. If the dog loses weight, then vegetable oil can be added. Veterinarians and behaviorists are having some success with pharmacology. In many cases treatment is possible and can improve the situation.

If you have done everything according to "the book" regarding training and socializing and are still having a behavior problem, don't procrastinate. It is important that the problem gets attention before it is out of hand. It is estimated that 20 percent of a veterinarian's time may be devoted to dealing with problems before they become so intolerable that the dog is separated from its home and owner. If your veterinarian isn't able to help, he should refer you to a behaviorist.

SUGGESTED READING

TS-213
Official Book of the Scottish Terrier
224 pages, over 100 full-color photos

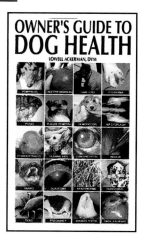

TS-214
Owner's Guide to Dog Health
224 pages, over 190 full-color photos

TS-252
Dog Behavior and Training
292 pages, over 200 full-color photos

TS-257
Choosing A Dog For Life
384 pages, over 700 full-color photos

INDEX